Cabinetmaking

Original title of the book in Spanish: *Ebanistería*

Published by Parramón Ediciones, S.A.,
Barcelona, Spain

Text: Vicenç Gibert and Josep López
Step-by-step: Eduard Vall-llosera
Series design: Carlos Bonet

Translated from the Spanish by Michael Brunelle and Beatriz Cortabarria.

All inquiries should be addressed to:
Barron's Educational Series, Inc.
250 Wireless Blvd.
Hauppauge, NY 11788
http://www.barronseduc.com

Library of Congress Catalog Card No. 00-101639
International Standard Book No. 0-7641-5242-4

Printed in Spain
9 8 7 6 5 4 3 2 1

TABLE OF CONTENTS

INTRODUCTION

The term *cabinetmaker* is used to describe a craftsman who is able to create furniture and decorative objects requiring a high level of skill, using fine woods like ebony, beech, oak, or rosewood. All cabinetmakers have a basic knowledge of, among other things, drafting and especially the techniques of assembling and joining wood and finishing it with varnishes, stains, and waxes.

If we look carefully at a piece of quality furniture, we will be able to appreciate that the piece itself is a summation of science, technology, skill, knowledge, and culture. A good cabinetmaker is one who is able to leave in his work the stamp of his personality that makes his pieces unique.

The art of cabinetmaking was already known to the ancient Egyptians, who worked with palm, sycamore, and ebony woods. The Greeks, Etruscans, and Romans were also magnificent cabinetmakers; they worked with such woods as olivewood, cedar, ebony, and boxwood to construct all types of furniture, which they adorned with silken fabrics, cushions, or inlaid gold, silver, and mother of pearl.

In Europe furniture became very important beginning with the fourteenth century, when carved decoration was used as an embellishment. In the fifteenth century sculptural motifs predominated. The seventeenth and eighteenth centuries witnessed the appearance of the styles of Louis XIV, Louis XV, and Louis XVI; during this time the urban middle class was buying this furniture, not the aristocracy. This glorious epoch—during which furniture evolved into artistic works of great style, elegance, and good taste—was followed by years of confusion that would last well into the nineteenth century, when heavy forms predominated.

In the United States during the mid-twentieth century, a type of functional furniture was born, with straight lines and without decoration. It opened the way to a new style that was not without a certain elegance.

The objective of this book is to introduce the wonderful craft of cabinetmaking, which captivates us with the smell, color, and texture of its basic material, wood, being shaped by hand. The subjects covered attempt to be a full introduction to the main materials and tools. If they do not turn out to be new to the expert, they certainly will be to the person who is just starting out or who will be working part-time at creating some type of furniture. The techniques presented are the fundamentals of the craft; they are the necessary skills used in creating objects or furniture that will show the fine touch of the cabinetmaker. Finally, the practical exercises show how to create the models step-by-step; these can be copied without too much effort, or modified according to one's needs or personal taste.

With this book, we wish to recognize and thank all of the anonymous cabinetmakers who through their work and great skill have helped make our daily surroundings a more pleasant and comfortable place.

Vicenç Gibert i Armengol

THE CRAFT OF THE CABINETMAKER

Originally, the term *cabinetmaker* was used to designate those persons whose trade was that of working with fine woods to create luxurious furniture for the nobility as well as other poweful clients.

Nowadays, cabinetmaking and carpentry are often confused, because both crafts involve working with the same raw materials. The main difference between the two rests in the type of wood that is used and in the amount of effort put into the final product. Therefore, while the carpenter usually uses common woods to construct simple chairs and the interiors of buildings, like door frames and windows, the cabinetmaker works with woods of a better quality to make furniture that requires more elaborate construction.

The cabinetmaker needs a spacious workshop where he or she can put a workbench and store different kinds of wood. The top of the workbench should have a tool well to hold the different tools; a bench dog—a wood wedge that allows quick bracing and holding of wood pieces—and a vise with a screw, which allows tight holding of any kind of wood. In the lower part of the bench, there is usually a shelf to hold the tools that are most often used; the smaller tools can be stored in a drawer. Besides the workbench, it is a good idea to have several sawhorses to support large pieces of wood.

The tools that cabinetmakers traditionally use have been improved over time and today allow them to work with wood more quickly and with greater precision than ever before. Along with saws and carpenter's planes, some of the most important tools have been the jack plane or bench plane, router plane, and the marking gauge; many are still in use today. At the same time, the incorporation of specific machines, like shapers and planers, has made an enormous difference in the amount of work that the master artisans must do.

1. In the old days, many furniture pieces were made of fine hardwoods, like this piece in solid ebony wood, with elegant decorative work.

2. A piece in the French style (1602–1672), also in solid ebony, where the extraordinary work of the cabinetmaker can be seen in the legs of the stand.

3. Isabelline-style chair in mahogany wood. The shaping of the front legs, the grooving in the backrest, and the carving of the back legs and backrest are outstanding.

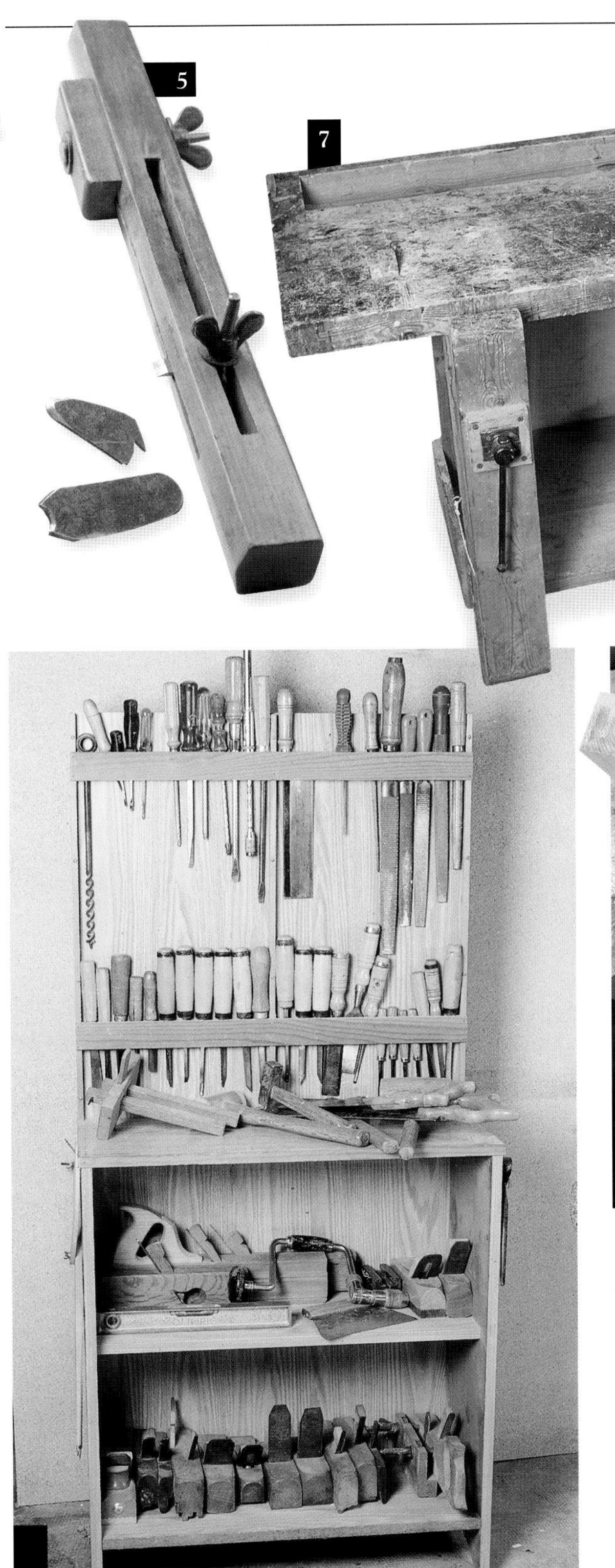

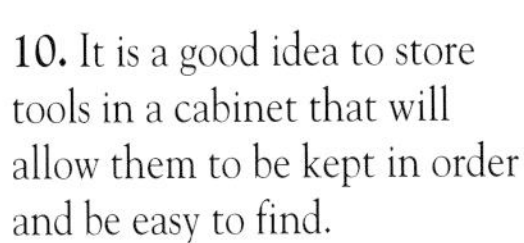

4. The marking gauge is a tool that cabinetmakers commonly use. It is used for marking parallel lines on a piece of wood.

5. The router plane is used for cutting grooves in the wood for the placement of inlay.

6. The rabbet plane is another tool traditionally used in cabinetmaking. It is used for cutting dados and rabbets in the wood.

7. The cabinetmaker's workbench should be made of thick wood that is resistant to wear because it has to support the weight of the furniture pieces and the action of the tools that are used for working the wood.

8. A vise is incorporated into the workbench to hold pieces of wood that are being worked.

9. The bench dog is a piece of wood inserted into the top of the workbench that acts as a stop for holding wood pieces.

10. It is a good idea to store tools in a cabinet that will allow them to be kept in order and be easy to find.

11. Besides the workbench, the cabinetmaker needs two or more sawhorses for holding and comfortably working with long boards.

ANALYSIS OF THE MATERIAL

There are innumerable kinds of trees that are used for their wood. Cabinetmakers usually work with hardwoods like walnut, cherry, beech, oak, mahogany, rosewood, ebony, or cedar. The prices of most of these woods are quite high. Softwoods, on the other hand, are not used because they are considered to be too soft; besides, they do not have attractive grain patterns and they lack coloring.

The cabinetmaker should be familiar with all of the woods, whether they are used in the form of solid material or veneers. Those woods that are most commonly used are listed below:

Fir. This is the lightest of the resinous woods. It has a long and straight grain structure, with wide annual rings. It is used to make the frames of furniture, boxes, and parts of musical instruments.

There is a marked difference between the wood from the spring and that from the fall. The knots are very dark and very hard, which is in contrast with the softness of the wood, and they often come loose from boards. If kept in a dry environment, the wood will last a long time; if kept in a poorly ventilated environment or one in which there are changes of temperature, the wood will easily rot.

Chestnut. This wood has a reddish ochre color. It has a pronounced grain structure and is strong and flexible. Full maturity is reached at eighty or one hundred years of age. It is very similar to oak, although it is much easier to work. A fine and luxurious appearance results from applying a glossy wax finish. It is very durable when it is in contact with water, but it is sensitive to air. It is used for many things, including fencing on farms, furniture, carts, and barrels.

Chestnut

Cherry

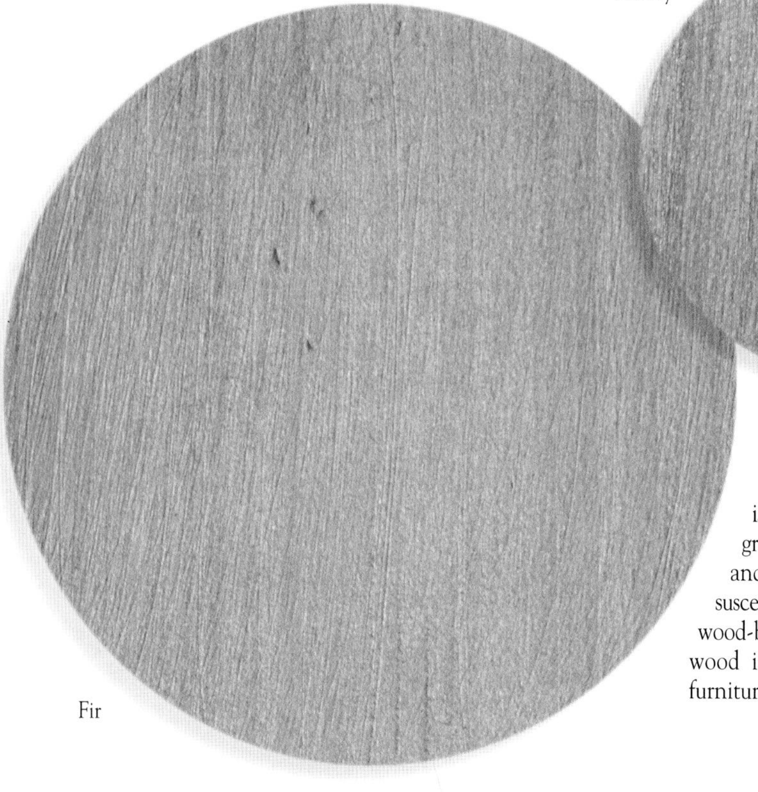

Fir

Cherry. This wood has a light chestnut color and is quite hard. It is easy to polish and stains well. The grain is quite straight and it shrinks. It is very susceptible to attacks by wood-boring insects. Cherry wood is primarily used for furniture.

Ash. This wood has a soft yellowish color, with a very attractive and straight grain pattern. It is dense, hard, durable, and one of the most flexible woods. It does not take stain well, but it can easily be cut and turned on the lathe. It will stay in perfect condition only if stored in a dry environment. It is most commonly used for furniture and for objects with curved shapes.

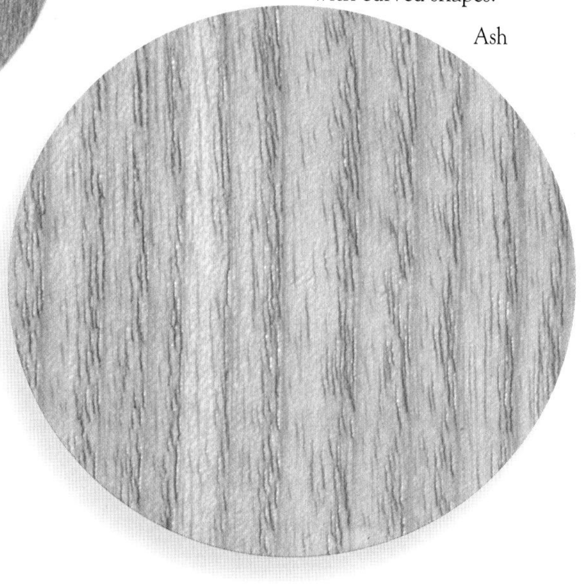

Ash

Walnut

Olivewood

Beech

Oak

Pine

European plane

Beech. This is a wood whose color is between yellow and white when it is young and soft red when it ages. It has a straight grain and homogenous structure, with few knots and many tissue marks in its core. It is heavy and flexible. It is susceptible to attack by wood-boring insects. Subject to twisting and rot, it is still one of the most widely used woods. It is used for constructing furniture that requires turned parts.

Olivewood. This is a yellowish wood with dark grain. It has a hard and compact structure, and it is long lasting. Easy to polish, it is used for things like works of art and luxury items.

Walnut. This wood has a brown color that darkens as it ages. It is of medium weight and has good structural strength. Its grain is compact, dense, and fine. It is easy to work and takes varnish well. Despite its susceptibility to moth infestation, it is one of the finest and most appreciated woods; it is used for producing veneer and making furniture, among other things.

Pine. A durable wood, it is very resinous, of a yellowish white color with a reddish grain. It gives off a turpentine smell, and it is very weather resistant. When the wood is of good quality, it is reserved for making furniture; when it is of lesser quality, it is used for household construction, boxes, and joinery.

Oak. A very slow-growing tree that produces wood of a yellowish brown color. It is known for its strength and its resistance to water; it gets harder when it comes in contact with water. Its grain structure is fine in radial cut boards. Used for making quality furniture, it is considered one of the best quality European woods.

European plane. This is a hard and heavy wood, similar in appearance to beech, but darker in color. It is easy to work on the lathe and is very susceptible to wood-boring insects. It is primarily used as veneer.

COMMONLY USED TOOLS

The tools that cabinetmakers use in their work can be classified, according to their function, as measuring and marking tools, cutting tools, shaping and smoothing tools, striking and pulling tools, drilling tools, and clamping tools.

Measuring and marking tools. Cabinetmakers usually begin a job by precisely measuring and marking the pieces that they are going to work. They have a series of instruments for this purpose, including some that the cabinetmakers make themselves.

Tools with cutting teeth. Commonly known as saws, the main characteristic of these tools is that they have a tempered steel blade, with triangular teeth. They work through back and forth movements; going forward they cut and going backward they assume their original position.

Tools with cutting blades. These include tools used for planing, removing material, or shaping pieces. Although all have cutting blades in common, these tools can be divided into two groups: those where the blade is held in a hardwood block, usually oak, and free-cutting tools that have a handle made of turned wood.

1. In a clockwise direction, beginning at the top: a compass, marking gauge, sliding bevel, try square, multiangle miter square, folding rule, and pencil. These are the most common measuring and marking tools.

2. The frame saw, the gent's saw, the tenon saw, and the common handsaw are the basic toothed cutting tools required in any cabinetmaker's shop.

3. The guided cutting tools have blades that are sharpened with a slightly concave bevel; they are grouped in two families, block planes and molding planes. Shown in the picture are some of these tools.

4. The chisel, the mortise chisel, and the gouge are free-cutting tools. They have a tempered steel blade sharpened on one end and brought to a point and inserted into a wooden handle at the other end.

Shaping and smoothing tools. Before finishing a piece of wood, a cabinetmaker refines it by shaping and smoothing it with tools such as files, scrapers, and sanders.

Striking and pulling tools. The main tools used for striking wood are hammers and mallets; for pulling nails or tacks, pincers.

Drilling tools. There are several tools available that can drill a hole in a piece of wood while causing little damage to the surface of the wood near the hole. These include drill bits, gimlets, and screwdrivers.

Clamping tools. While some type of glue is required to join different pieces of wood, a clamp that tightly presses the pieces together must be used while the glue sets. These tools have many different names, including press, screw clamp, vise, clamp, and holdfast.

5. Different types of files (half-round, round, and rasp).

6. From left to right: nylon mallet, carpenter's hammer, wooden mallet, cabinetmaker's hammer, veneering hammer, and flat pin hammer.

7. Drill bits, gimlets, and screwdrivers are tools that are used for making holes in wood. The carpenter's brace is a handle that can be used with different types of bits.

8. Pliers and pincers are steel tools consisting of two movable arms attached by a rivet. They are mainly used for pulling nails. The nail set is a tool that has a pointed steel rod used for setting nails.

9. The frame clamp or corner clamp is used to hold corners that have been glued. The web clamp or circular clamp is used when gluing a round piece, and the cabinetmaker's clamp is used when gluing two pieces together.

SHARPENING AND POLISHING TOOLS

The cutting tools used in cabinetmaking suffer indisputable wear and tear from use. Sometimes, the damage comes from striking materials of a greater hardness, which causes dents. It is both practical and economical for a cabinetmaker to sharpen and tune his or her own tools; therefore, a few methods are explained to keep the tools in optimum condition.

Sharpening

Sharpening consists of grinding the tool's worn out cutting blade.

For the blades of planes, chisels, mortise chisels, and gouges, a cabinetmaker uses a grinder with a sharpening wheel—a synthetic stone (for example, emery) that rotates at great speed, producing friction on the blade. In the old days, grindstones made of natural stone were used; these rotated very slowly and were kept wet.

Saws are sharpened with files. The saw is held in place on the workbench with the vise and the teeth are ground with the file.

Scrapers are sharpened with a burnisher, a kind of triangular file without markings, which is completely smooth. By pressing the burnisher against the scraper, a cabinetmaker can create a hook along the edge.

Honing

After sharpening, the blade is honed to eliminate the burr, to create a better edge. Honing is done with a polishing stone impregnated with oil. The beveled side and the backside of the blade are honed on the polishing stone in turn, making a figure-eight movement.

Setting

After the teeth of a saw have been sharpened, the blade goes through the process of setting, to prevent them from catching or binding. Using a tool called a saw set, the cabinetmaker bends the teeth alternately, one to the right and one to the left. This process is done so the width of the cut is bigger than the thickness of the cutting blade, thus keeping the saw from getting entangled.

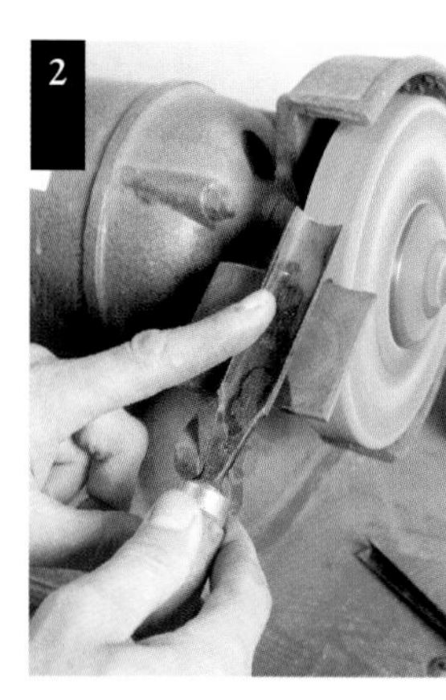

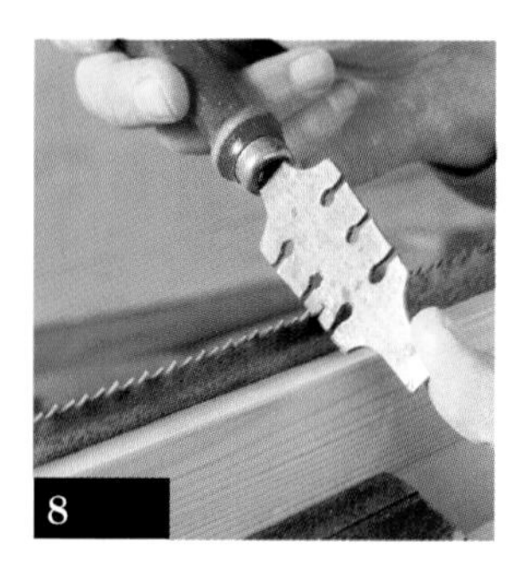

1. Sharpening a chisel with an emery grindstone. The tool should be braced firmly on the support plate of the machine.

2. Sharpening a gouge with an emery grindstone.

3. Sharpening a mortise chisel with an emery grindstone. The tool should first be submerged in water to prevent it from overheating and burning.

4. Sharpening a saw with a triangular file.

5. Sharpening a scraper blade with a burnisher.

6 and **7.** To hone the blade of a plane, the beveled side is pressed firmly on the sharpening stone, which has been impregnated with oil, and sharpened by making figure-eight movements. Then, the same is done with the backside of the blade.

8. Setting the teeth of a saw with a saw set.

MAKING THE DRAWING

The first thing that must be done when beginning a cabinetmaking project is to design the object that is going to be made.

Sometimes, a simple sketch is sufficient. But to be precise, it is advisable to prepare a scale drawing from which to measure the different pieces.

If the project is of large scale, it is best to make a full-sized working drawing to lay out over a wood board; this way, it will be easier and more comfortable for the cabinetmaker to take measurements.

In some cases, the cabinetmaker may decide to lay out the plan of the project directly on the board, which will serve as a pattern, or on the wood pieces that will be used to help in fitting the parts that will make up the furniture piece.

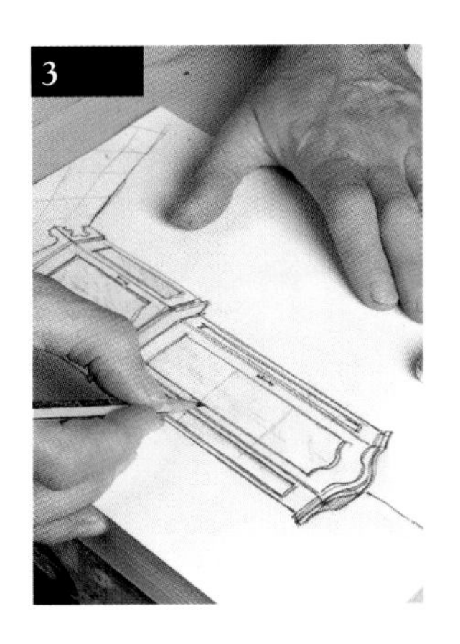

1. A color print, such as the one of this giraffe, can be used as a model for what the cabinetmaker wishes to project on wood.

2. From the photograph, the cabinetmaker produces the working drawing, which will be used to plan all the required parts of the object.

3. If the project has been commissioned, it is advisable to produce a sketch on paper so the client can get an idea of what the object will look like.

4. Full-scale working drawing on paper with all the parts required for a wood box.

5. Drawing of a wheel on a wood board. On top of it are the marking tools needed for making it: a pencil, a try square, a folding rule, and dividers.

SAWING AND WORKING WOOD

The cabinetmaker usually purchases long, large pieces of wood with approximate surface measurements of 4 × 12 inches (10 × 30 cm) and lengths that vary between 6 and 30 feet (2 and 10 m). In a case such as this, the wood must be cut and surfaced to obtain the appropriate dimensions. However, wood that is already cut to different sizes is now available commercially, which makes the cabinetmaker's job much easier.

In the old days, the surfacing of the wood was done with a carpenter's plane and a jack plane, tools that are still used even today. When working with one of these tools, a cabinetmaker must hold the wood or attach it to the workbench, using clamps or a bench vise.

The appearance of the first woodworking machines was a great technological advance that allowed more precision and speed in the construction of fine wood furniture. Of all of them, the jointer and the thickness planer deserve special mention. The characteristic they have in common is that their cutting blades are attached to a cylinder. The difference between the two machines is in their use: The jointer is used in the first phase to smooth out the sides and corners of the wood that is to be worked; the thickness planer is used later to give the piece the specific surface dimensions.

The wood can also be cut into sections or sawed. This task is basically done with a single tool, a saw. The saw can be used for a variety of techniques that make a cabinetmaker's job much easier.

To saw manually, the piece of wood can be rested on a stool, placing the knee over it to hold it in place. The wood can also be attached to the workbench using a press or the bench dog as a stop. Nevertheless, it is advisable to use a cutting guide, which the cabinetmaker can make. This guide consists of a flat piece of wood with a wood bar that is attached to the workbench and another bar that is used to hold the wood that is to be sawed.

For projects that require a more precise technique, either stationary or portable power saws can be used. The most common ones are the band saw, the circular or table saw, the miter saw, and the jigsaw.

1. Using a jack plane to plane down the edge of a door. Notice that the door is held up with a base consisting of notched boards.

2. The jointer consists of a base and two cast-iron tables, a steel cylinder where the cutting blades are housed, and a motor.

3. The thickness planer consists of a large cast-iron box where all the mechanisms are housed. It is much easier to use than the jointer.

4. Hand sawing with a common saw, while resting the knee on the wood to hold it in place.

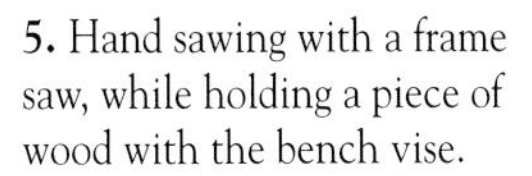

5. Hand sawing with a frame saw, while holding a piece of wood with the bench vise.

6. Sawing manually with a tenon saw, holding the wood against a bench dog on the workbench.

7. Sawing manually with a tenon saw, resting the wood on a cutting miter guide attached to the bench vise.

8. Sawing a wood board mechanically with a band saw.

9. Sawing wood mechanically with a table saw.

10. Sawing wood mechanically with a miter saw.

11. Sawing wood mechanically with a portable jigsaw.

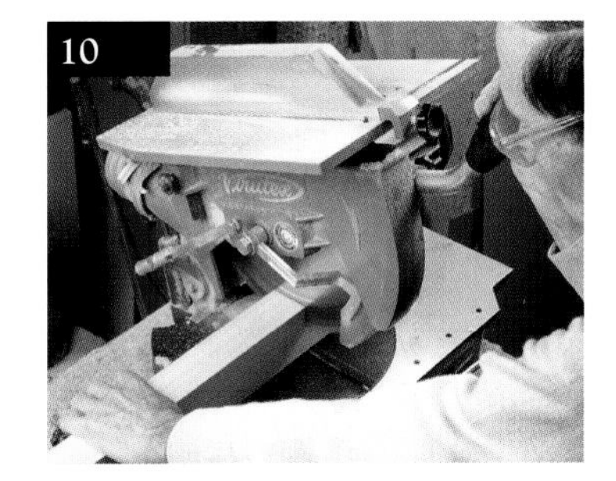

PATTERN MAKING AND MARKING

Once the wood has been dimensioned, the cabinetmaker marks it.

With patterns, the task of marking can be repeated as many times as needed. Although patterns can be made of different materials, the ones made of wood are the most common, and they are easy to make.

To create patterns, different parts of the furniture can be drawn on several boards or on a single board. Tracing paper can also be used as a sort of carbon paper. Once the drawing is finished, the cabinetmaker can begin sawing and shaping the pattern.

In some cases, it is not necessary to use a pattern: Marking can be done directly on the wood, for example, when cutting up boards for making several wood blanks that will be used to make identical parts, or when cutting boards to length.

When making patterns, the cabinetmaker uses different marking and tracing tools, for example, the compass, beam compass, and the square. The jigsaw, which is easy to operate, is used to cut and shape the pattern once it is drawn. Marking straight and parallel lines is done with the marking gauge. To see the lines better, the cabinetmaker retraces with a pencil the marks that the tool made.

When marking rough boards, a carpenter's pencil is used, with a flat graphite point. When marking joints on fine woods, a fine-point pencil is preferable.

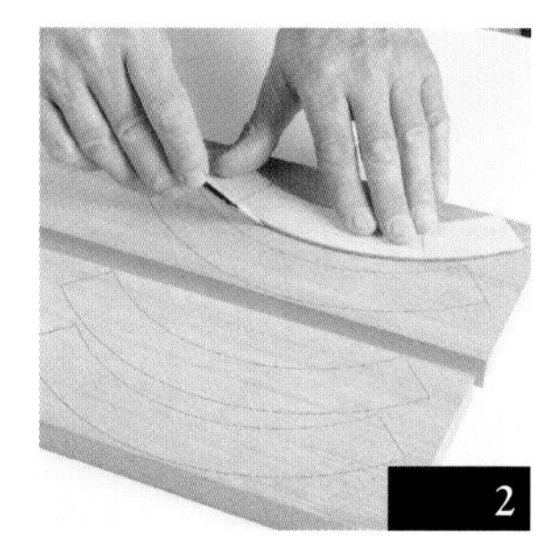

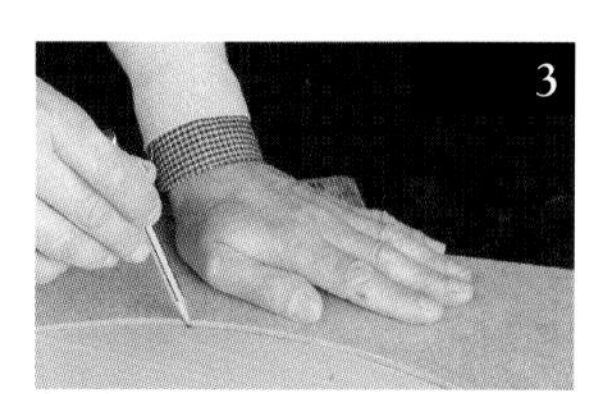

1. Tracing a pattern on a board by laying it over a working drawing.

2. Using the same pattern to draw several pieces, while making the best use of the wood.

3. When marking with medium-sized patterns, the pattern should be held in place with one hand while tracing with the other.

4. Marking curved shapes on a board with the help of some nails and a strip of flexible wood, which allows the cabinetmaker to mark the various curves with a pencil.

5. A very large curved shape can be traced using a simple tool in the shape of an arch, which can be made larger or smaller depending on the tension of the cord.

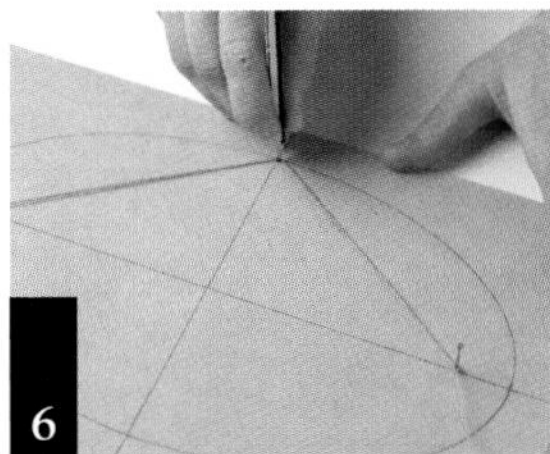

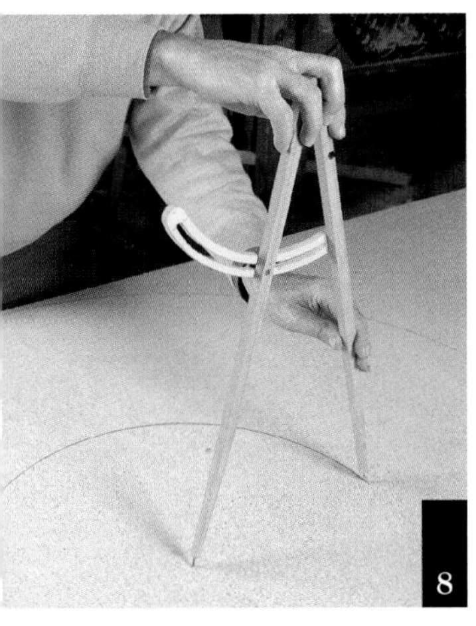

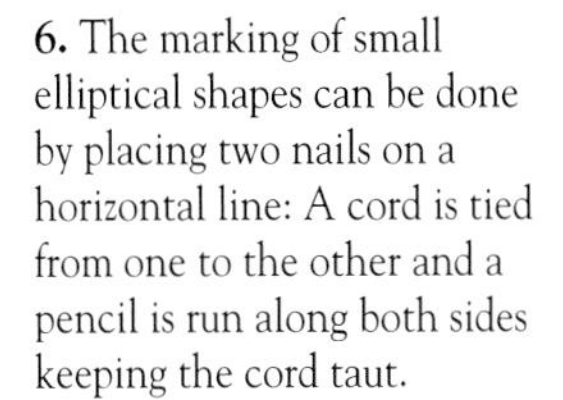

6. The marking of small elliptical shapes can be done by placing two nails on a horizontal line: A cord is tied from one to the other and a pencil is run along both sides keeping the cord taut.

7. The marking of large elliptical shapes can be done with more sophisticated or clever methods, such as the one shown in the picture. This method uses two double strips of wood in the shape of a cross and a third one that slides over them, allowing the cabinetmaker to draw different elliptical shapes.

8. Marking a circle with a wooden compass.

9. A beam compass must be used to mark circles with large diameters.

10. Numbering the pieces and marking them with an "X" will help when pairing boards.

11. The cabinetmaker is able to draw perfectly straight lines with a pencil by bracing the middle and ring fingers against the edge of the board.

12. Parallel lines can be drawn quickly by holding the wood firmly and by using a try square and a measuring tape.

JOINERY

On many occasions it is necessary for the cabinetmaker to add on one or more boards to arrive at the required dimensions.These additions can be done in two different ways: by joining one board to another to make it wider or by scarfing or splicing one board to another to make it longer.

The word *joint* refers to the union of two pieces to each other at an angle.

Edge Joining

When the wood chosen for a particular project is not the required length, width, or thickness, two or more pieces must be joined using nails, screws, or glue.

In edge joining, it is important to pay attention to the expanding and contracting movements of the wood caused by its levels of humidity. Therefore, the points where the wood is joined should be reinforced in the manner most appropriate to the project.

The most commonly used joints are:

Loose-tongue joint. The grain of the wood that acts as the tongue should run contrary to the boards to increase the strength of the joint. A grooving plane is used to make the grooves in the boards.

This type of joint is used for joining very thick boards, so that the grooves do not weaken the walls.

Glued shiplap joints. This type of joint greatly resists the movements of the wood because it has a lot of surface contact but no weak points caused by removing wood. This joint is cut using a rabbet plane.

Butt joint with butterfly keys. This is characterized as a self-locking or clamping joint. It is one of the most traditional ways of joining wood.

Biscuit joint. The biscuits are made of compressed wood fibers. They are used for small furniture joints that do not have to resist movement.

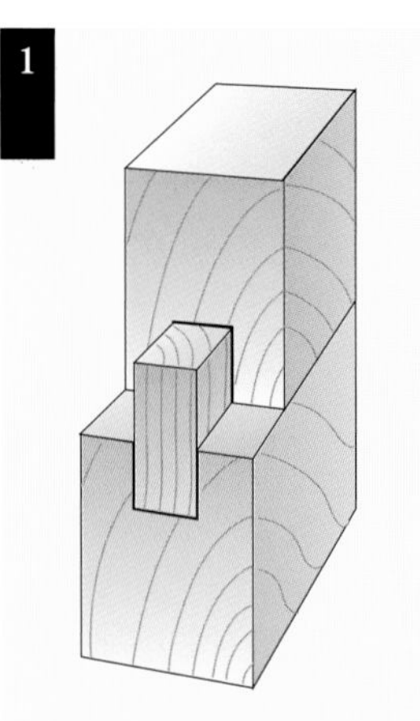

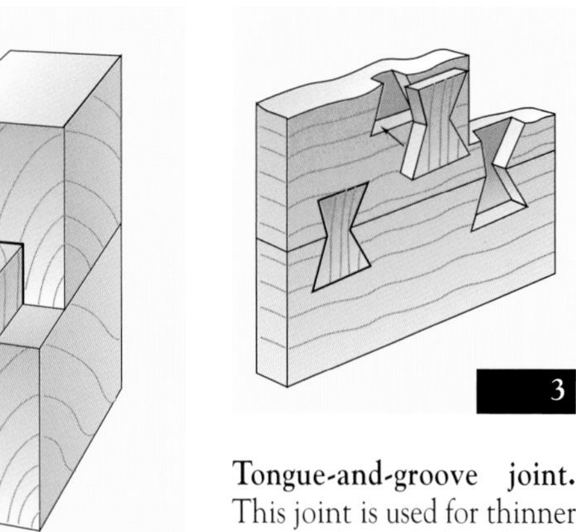

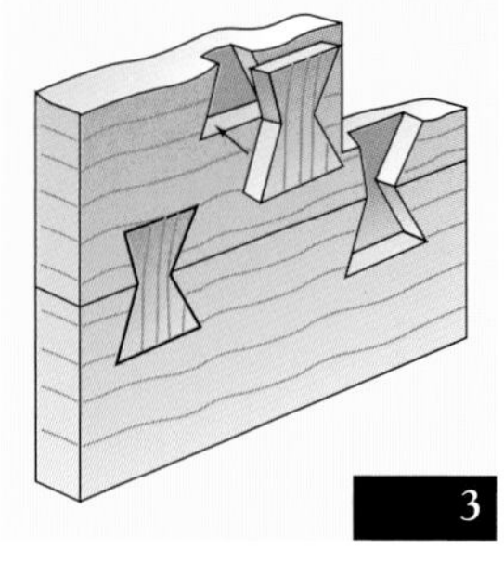

Tongue-and-groove joint. This joint is used for thinner pieces of wood that do not have to withstand any great force. A combination plane is required to make this type of joint.

Tongue-and-groove joint with beveled corners. The combination plane with its tongue cutter and matching plowing cutter should be used to cut the tongue and groove, and a block plane should be used to make the beveled edge. Notice how

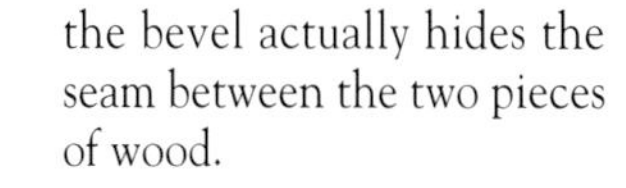

the bevel actually hides the seam between the two pieces of wood.

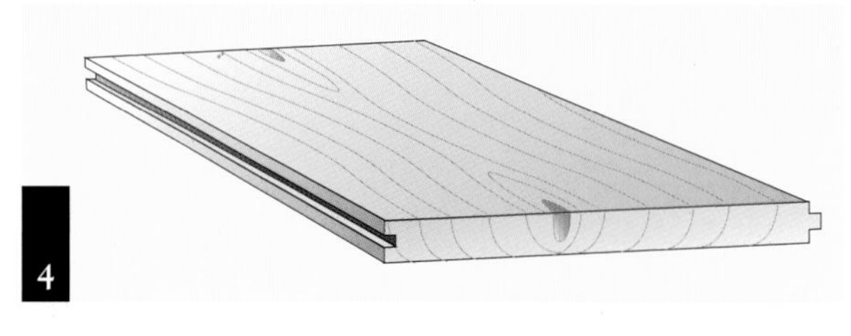

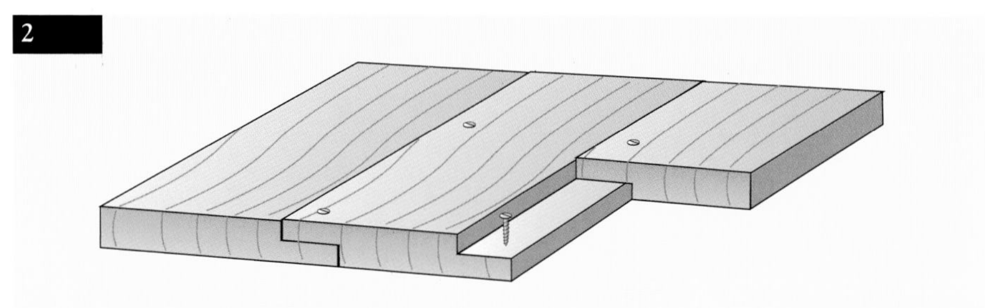

1. Loose tongue joint.

2. Shiplap joint.

3. Butt joint with butterfly keys.

4. Tongue-and-groove joint.

5. Tongue-and-groove joint with beveled corners.

6. Biscuit joint.

Scarf Joints

Scarfing, or splicing, consists of joining two pieces of wood at their ends, resulting in a single piece of wood of greater length. Generally, cabinetmakers do not have to use scarfing, because large pieces of furniture are made with parts that can be disassembled and the wood used is usually of sufficient length.

However, if scarfing is needed, the type of scarf used will depend on whether the forces that the wood must support are vertical or horizontal, on the face or on the edge, under tension or compression forces. Normally, joined wood pieces are not as strong as single integral pieces.

The most commonly used scarfs are:

Half-lapped scarf. This is the simplest of the scarf joints that cabinetmakers use. Half of the material is removed from the ends, and they are placed one over the other. The joint is then reinforced with screws or bolts.

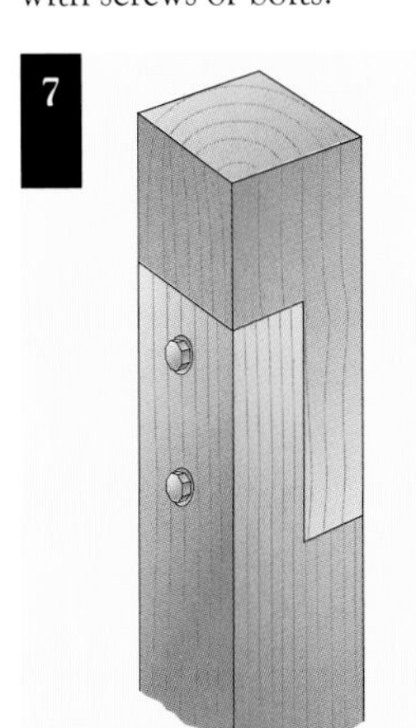

Squint-butted scarf. The length of the cut is always two or three times longer than the width of the piece. The scarf is reinforced with screws, brads, or fasteners.

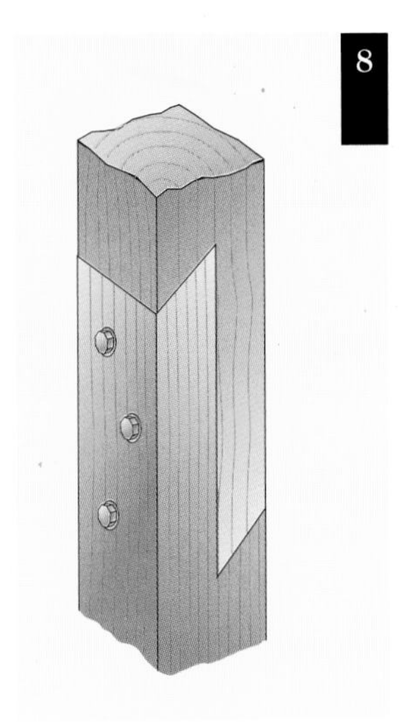

Tenon scarf. This can be done with a cut tenon or with dowels. The length and diameter of the dowel must be in proportion to the section of the wood pieces.

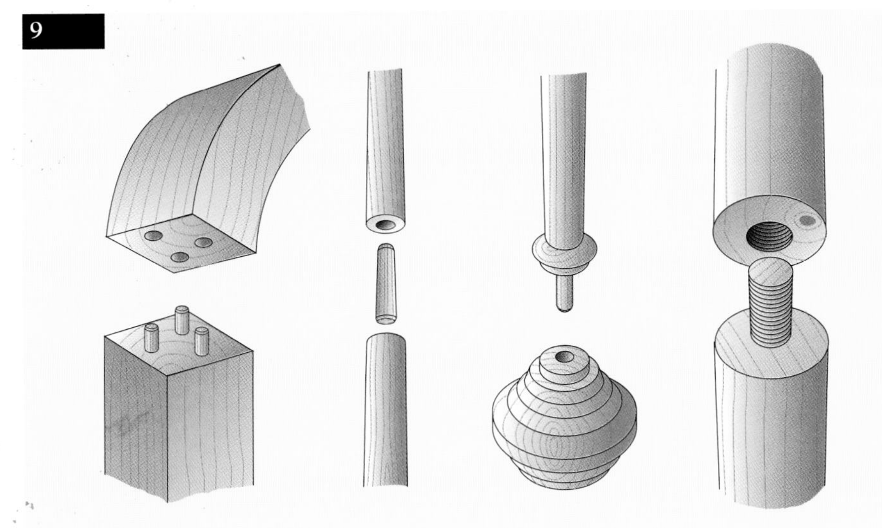

Bridle scarf. When the cuts are made accurately, this is a solid joint. The thickness of the tenon should be around one-third of the thickness of the wood.

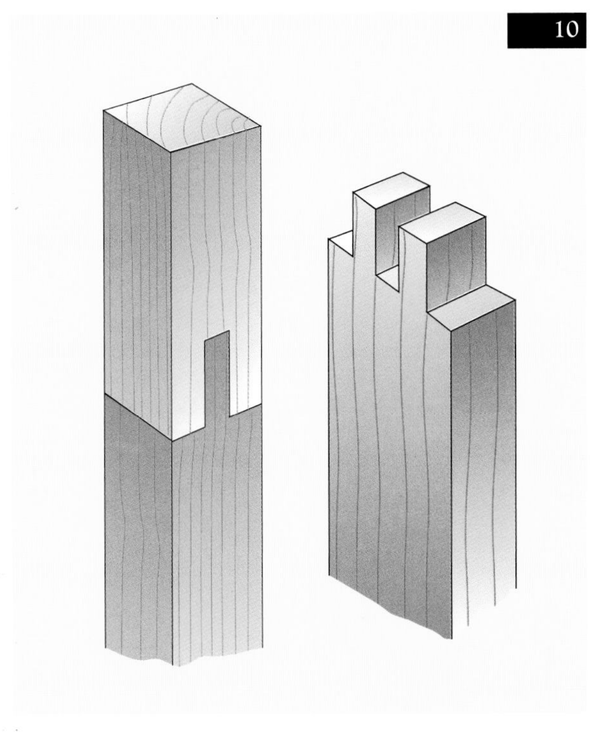

Finger scarf. This scarf can be quite strong if well executed and quality adhesives are used. It is not recommended for pieces that will be under compression.

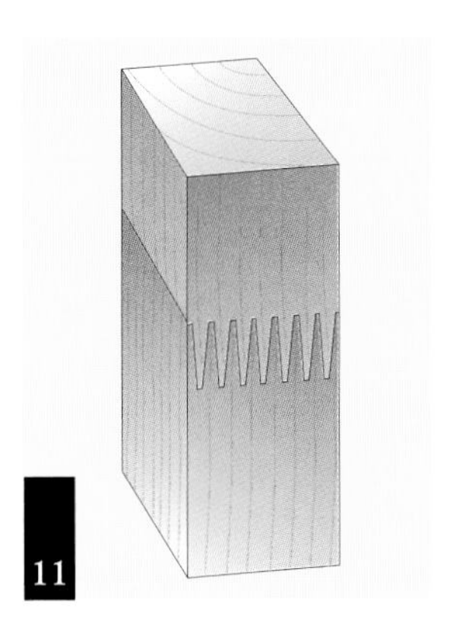

Dovetail-key scarf. This is one of the most appropriate joints for boards under tension. The tenon is left unglued. When placed on edge it will resist flexing forces well.

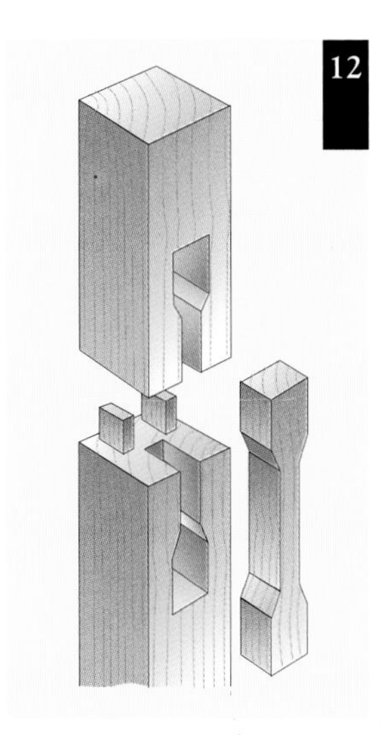

7. Half-lapped scarf.

8. Squint-butted scarf.

9. Tenon scarf.

10. Bridle scarf.

11. Finger scarf.

12. Dovetail-key scarf.

Joints

Two pieces of wood can be joined at an angle in one of two ways. The first consists of perfectly smoothing the ends of the boards that will be joined, gluing them together, and holding them under pressure until the glue dries. The second method, known as joinery or joining, consists of cutting a groove called a mortise in one of the boards and a tenon or tongue in the other so that they fit together perfectly. Both the groove and the tongue should be made in the middle part of the pieces that will be joined together.

Traditionally, joints have always been made using a hand tool such as a chisel, mallet, gouge, or tenon saw. However, now there are special machines commercially available that make this task easier for the cabinetmaker.

The most common types of joints are:

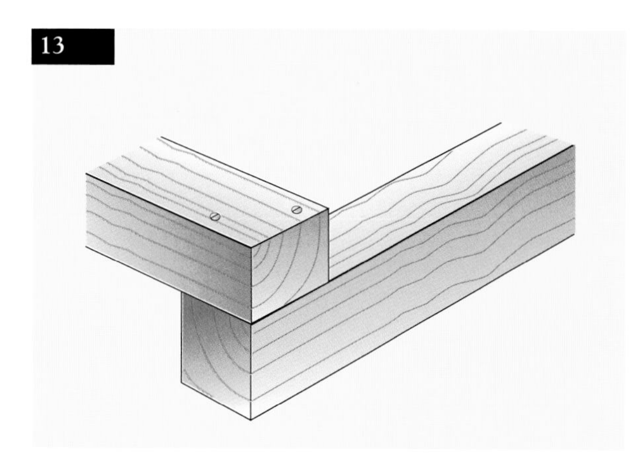

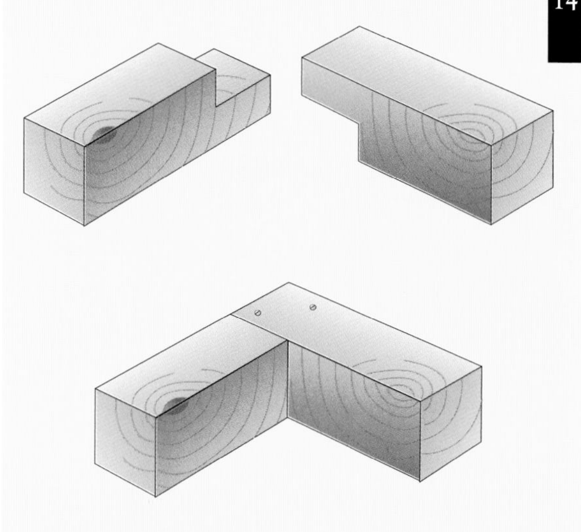
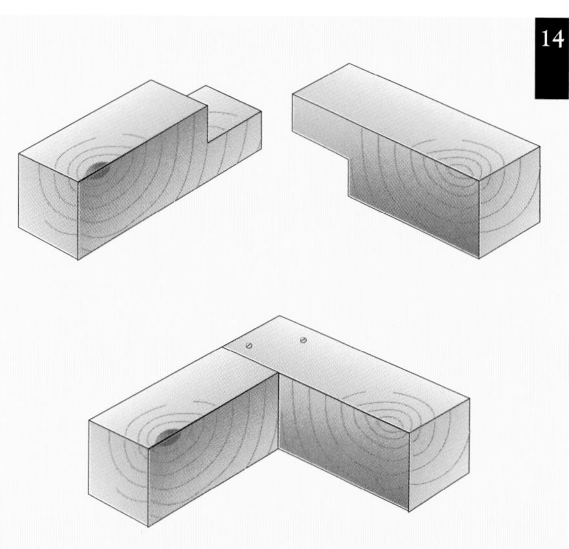

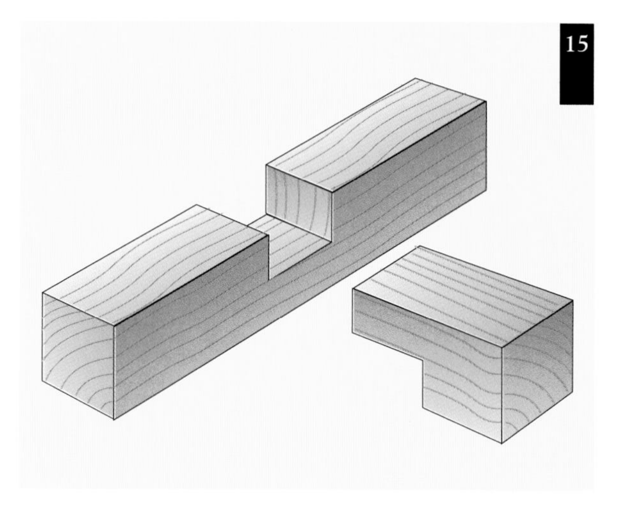

Lap joint. This is the simplest of all joints. It is done using nails, brads, or screws and glue.

End lap or L-lap joint. In this type of joint, half the thickness of the wood is cut away with a small saw. The pieces can be attached with glue or using small nails.

T-lap joint. In this type of joint, one of the pieces is inserted into the opening made in the other piece.

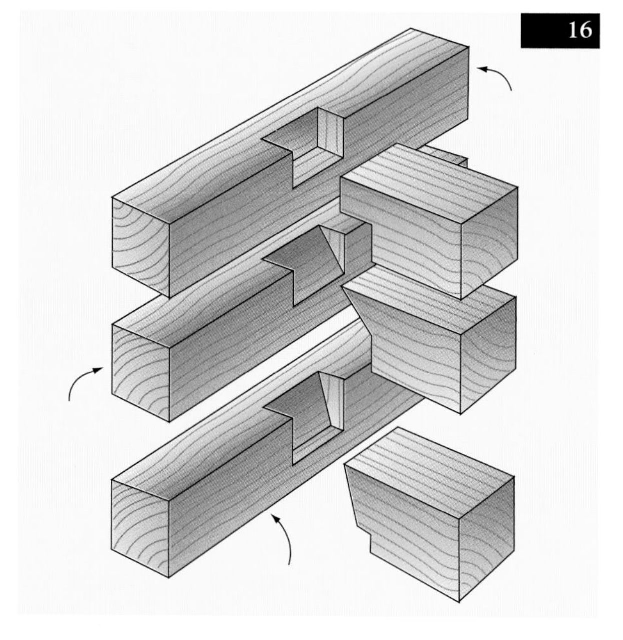

Dovetail lap joint. The name of this joint comes from its similarity to the shape of a dove's tail. It is normally used for joints that must sustain a high level of tension.

13. Lap joint.

14. End lap or L-lap joint.

15. T-lap joint.

16. Housed lap joints. These are variations of the T-lap joint.

17. Dovetail lap joint. This is another variation of the T-lap joint.

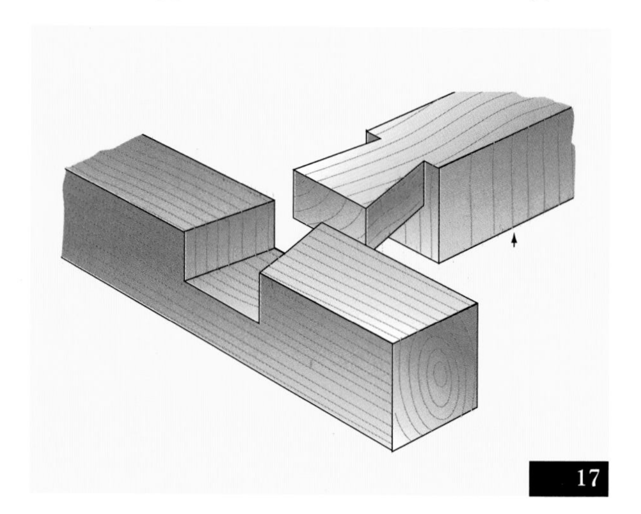

Through pin dovetail lap joint. This differs from the dovetail lap joint because it is more resistant to twisting and flexing pressure than to tension.

Mitered butt joint with inset angle brace. This type of joint usually has an angle brace attached with screws or nails to reinforce the joint.

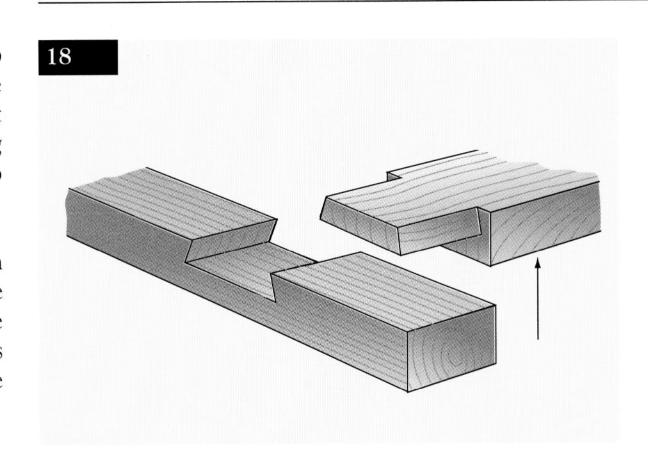

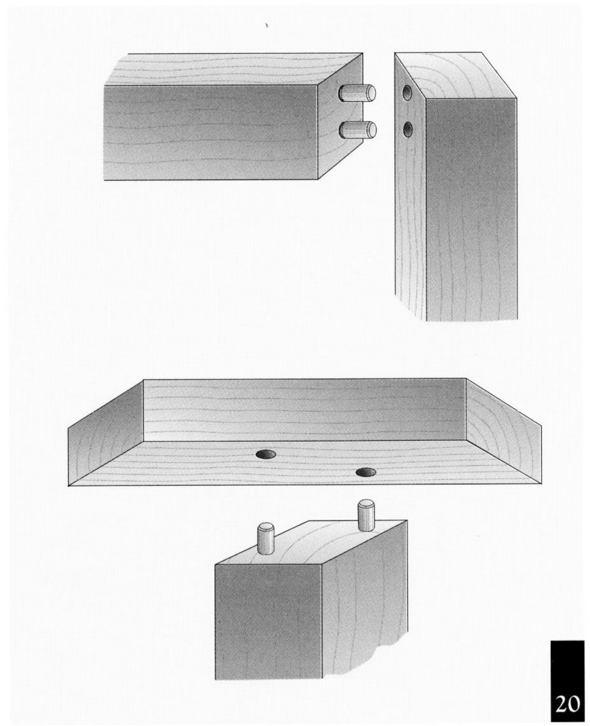

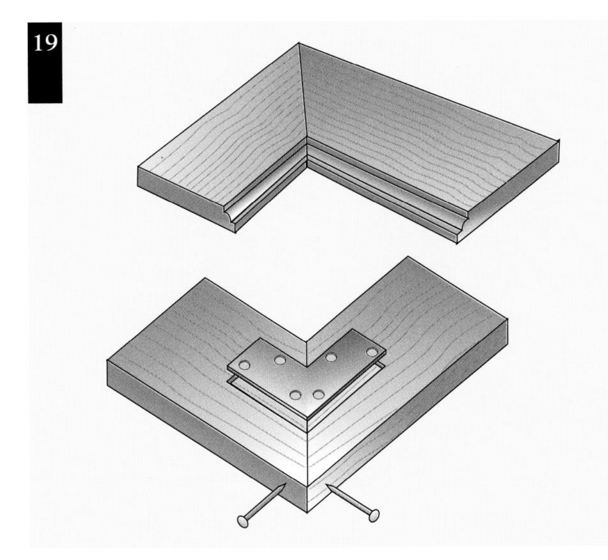

Mitered butt joint with dowels. This is very similar to the previous joint, but with a 45-degree angle cut that allows the parts to be joined at their ends.

Through mortise and tenon joint. The name refers to the fact that the tenon is inserted into a mortise that is cut completely through the piece of wood. When the mortise does not go through the wood it is called a blind mortise.

Blind dovetail joint. The strength of this joint comes from the fit of multiple pins and dovetails. With this joint, the boards can be either the same or different thicknesses.

Doweled butt joint. The dowels are always fitted snugly, and many have grooves, or fluting, along the sides to make the glue adhere better.

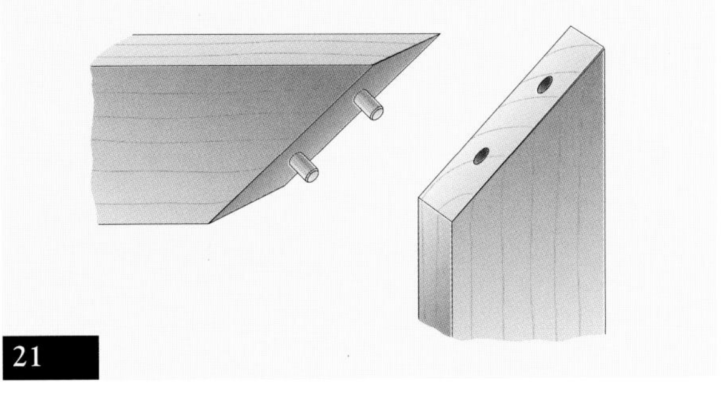

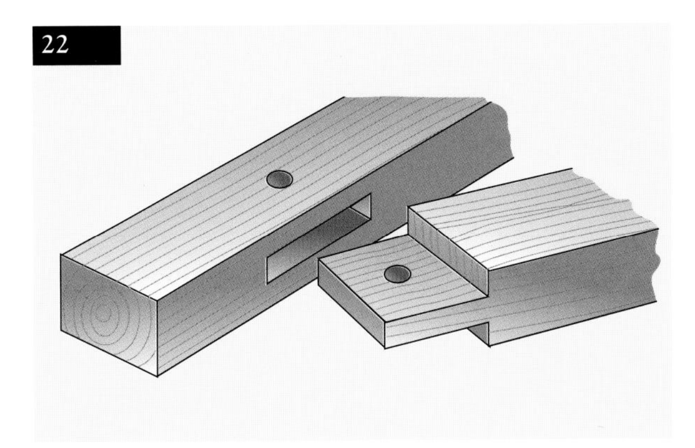

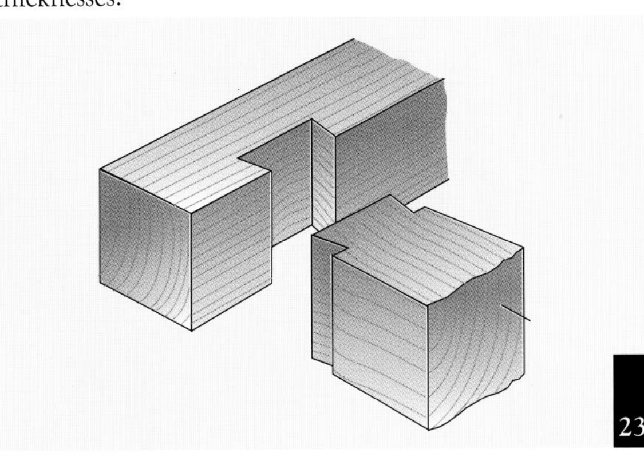

18. Through pin dovetail lap joint.

19. Mitered butt joint with inset angle brace.

20. Doweled butt joints.

21. Mitered butt joint with dowels.

22. Through mortise and tenon joint.

23. Blind dovetail joint.

VENEERING

Veneering consists of covering a piece of furniture with thin sheets of wood. It is a purely decorative operation that gives the bench-made furniture pieces a more beautiful, luxurious appearance.

The veneers are sheets of wood about 1/28 inch (1 mm) thick. In theory, all the trees used for carpentry projects can be used to make veneer.

In the old days, furniture was made of solid wood, and veneer was only added to improve the quality of some of its parts; this was done using marquetry techniques, which use veneers of different colors, in different arrangements. However, nowadays, veneer is usually used to conceal the fiberboard that the furniture is made of, because a surface made of cherry or oak is far more pleasant and attractive to the eye.

A special veneer saw or a blade with a sharp edge can be used to cut sheets of veneer. Using certain shears reduces the amount of time needed for the task, and it is more precise. No matter which tool is chosen for the purpose, the cabinetmaker must proceed with caution because the sheet breaks easily, especially if the cut is made across the wood grain.

When several pieces of veneer are used, the pieces are held together temporarily with adhesive tape. Although it is sufficient to place tape only at some of the joining points, if a perfect fit is desired, adhesive tape should be placed along the entire length.

The pieces can be bonded with contact cement or white glue. When using contact cement, apply it to both surfaces and wait for five minutes until the glue is dry to the touch; next, bond both pieces together by applying even pressure to them. A veneering hammer, whose surface is large enough to press any sheet, may be used for this task. When using white glue for bonding veneer, the surfaces must be clamped for about two hours.

Finally, the sheet should be sanded or scraped to achieve a smoother finish. It can also be stained and varnished.

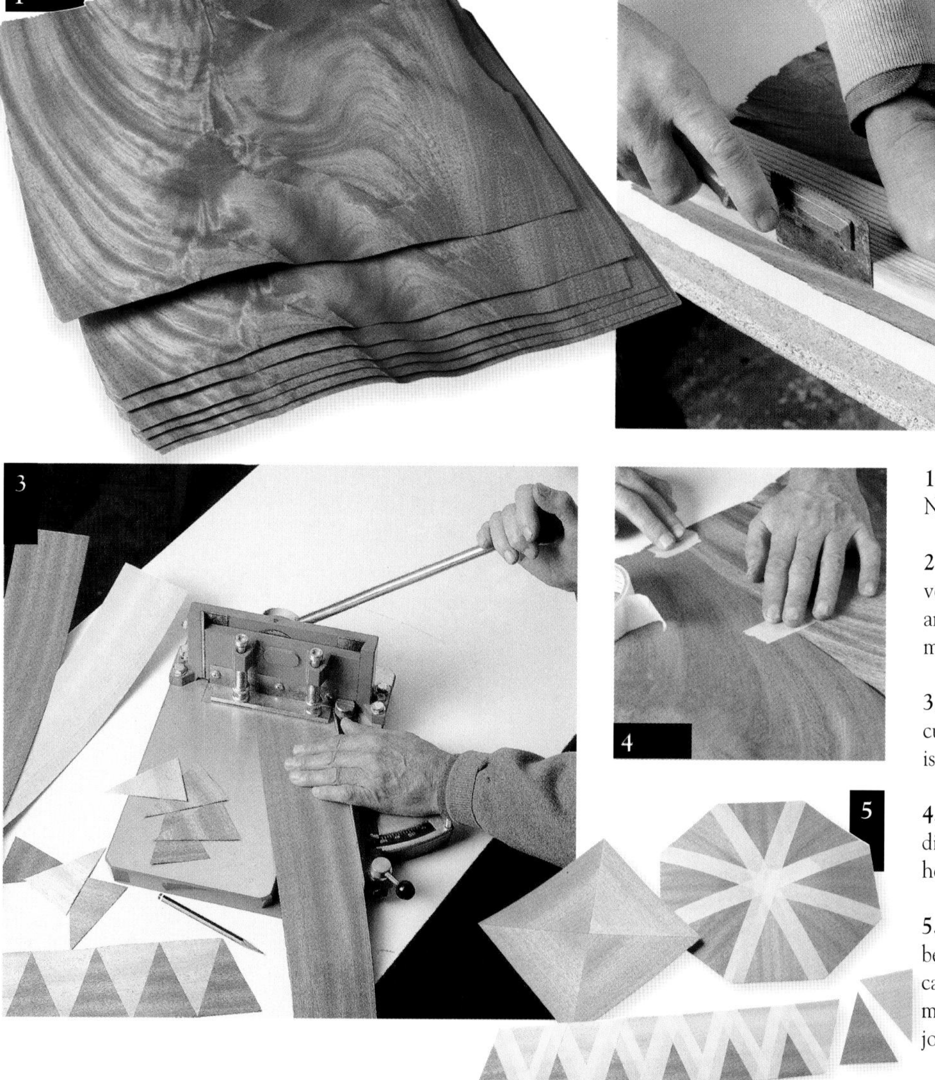

1. Sheets of veneer cut in squares. Notice how thin they are.

2. The cabinetmaker uses a veneering saw to cut the veneer and a wooden ruler as a guide for making straight cuts.

3. When the veneer is cut with curtain shears, the resulting cut is cleaner and more precise.

4. Masking tape can be used at different points of the seam to hold two pieces together.

5. To achieve better fit and to better place the pieces, a cabinetmaker will place masking tape along the entire joint of the piece.

6. To achieve a good bond, contact cement should be applied to both the surface of the veneer and the base.

7 and **8.** When enough time has elapsed for the contact cement to dry to the touch, the pieces are put together.

9. The entire glued surface can be pressed very efficiently with the veneering hammer.

10. The surface of the veneer is sanded after gluing.

11. Veneer of different combined colors is used to decorate furniture.

12. Radial matched veneers for round tabletops.

ASSEMBLY AND GLUING

Assembly is one of the most important steps in constructing a piece of furniture. Its durability and proper functioning depend on how well it is assembled.

Before a cabinetmaker can assemble a piece of furniture, all the wood parts should be properly cut, shaped, and, most important, sanded. Clearly, it is more efficient to sand a piece of wood furniture before assembly, when it is much easier to reach all of the surfaces.

When assembling a piece of furniture, there are basically two ways of joining the parts: one using joints and glue and the other using any type of nails and screws. It is recommended that the cabinetmaker master the skills of making all types of joints.

When working with joints, a cabinetmaker should keep in mind that the joints made using dowels rather than cut tenons simplify the process. The various pieces of wood are bonded with white glue, using a clamp to exert pressure on them. If white glue is to be used, before the assembly and the permanent gluing begins, a dry assembly must be done. This consists of putting all the pieces together, even using clamps exactly as if glue were being used; this way the cabinetmaker can detect possible errors and correct them before the wood becomes stained with glue.

When working with mechanical fasteners, a cabinetmaker should know the different types of screws that are available on the market to allow for a wider range of possibilities.

Finally, a cabinetmaker should also keep in mind that assembly with joints and glue makes a later disassembly difficult and assembly with mechanical fasteners makes a later disassembly quicker, which makes transporting the piece much easier. Nevertheless, it is worth noting that the majority of the furniture that comes out of the factory is partly glued and partly assembled with mechanical fasteners.

1. Before the cabinetmaker begins assembling the piece of furniture, all the materials should be prepared and the wood perfectly sanded.

2. Using glued dowels to join two pieces is an easy method.

3. To place the dowels properly, they must be inserted in the holes made in the part and their length marked using a piece of wood. Then the excess piece can be cut off easily.

4. It is preferable to use glue for attaching molding.

5. After gluing, the pieces should be held under pressure. In the case of the previously mentioned molding, placing a 2-lb. (1-kg) weight on it is sufficient.

6. Gluing the dowels for an armchair made of teak.

7. After gluing, pressure must be applied to the joints. In this case, clamps will be used.

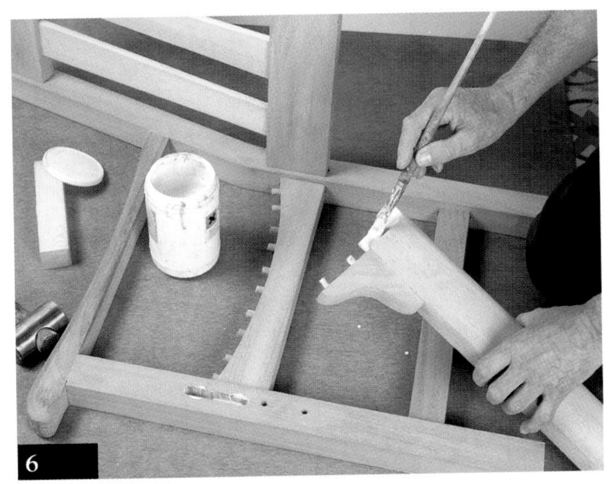

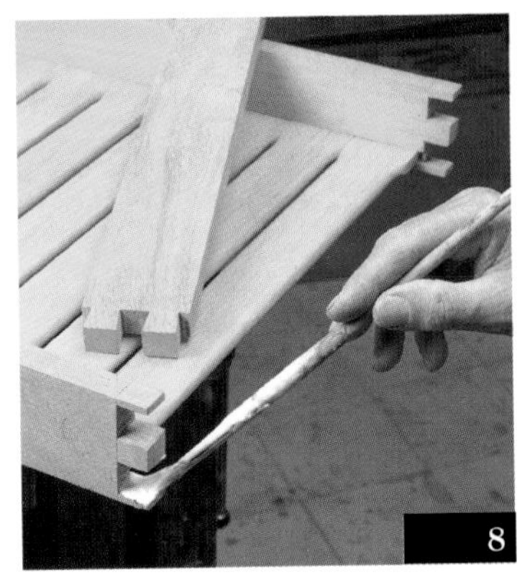

8. If the joints are made using glue and dovetails, there is no need to apply pressure on them.

9. Hinges are an example of mechanical fasteners.

10. Sometimes, the cabinetmaker may join two pieces with screws. Using them makes disassembly easier.

11. In some pieces, such as the hub of a wheel for example, the use of screws is necessary.

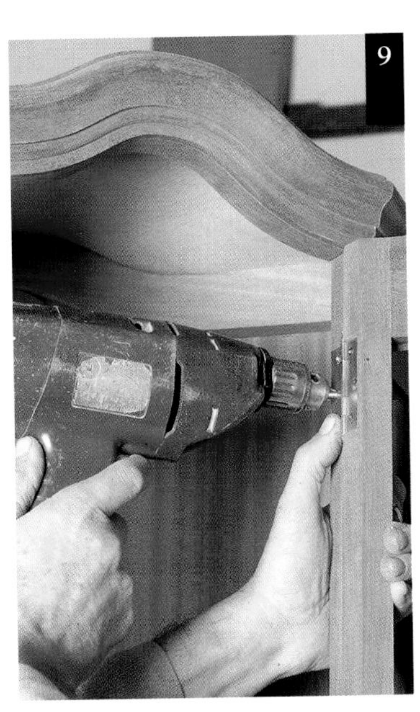

SANDING, FILING, AND SCRAPING

Sanding, filing, and scraping are three ways to create a better finish on the wood.

Sanding, as its name indicates, consists of rubbing sandpaper over the surface of the wood. There are many types of sandpaper whose basic difference is the grit, which ranges from coarse to fine; the finer the grit, the smoother the finish achieved.

Sanding can be done manually or mechanically. When doing it manually, wrapping the sandpaper around a block of wood makes the process easier. When doing it mechanically, there are two types of power sanders that can be used: the belt sander, with a continuous strip of sandpaper, and the orbital sander, with a vibrating movement. The orbital sander is normally used to sand surfaces that have already been varnished.

Filing is the task that usually follows sawing. It is a good way to achieve the desired shapes and curves. Different types of files are used to perform this task: flat, half-round, cylindrical, and triangular. Each will be used according to the desired outcome. The file is held by its handle with one hand; the end of the file is held with the other hand to apply further pressure on the wood.

The difference between a file and a rasp is that the latter is coarser and allows more material to be removed from the wood.

Scraping, or smoothing, is done with a scraper, a tool that consists of a steel blade, rectangular in shape, with a sharpened edge on its longer side. It is held with both hands, flexing it while scraping the wood, which produces small shavings.

Generally, in order to carry out the sanding, filing, and scraping comfortably, the wood must be firmly attached to the workbench.

1. Sanding the flat surface of the wood with sandpaper wrapped around a wood block. When doing this, the cabinetmaker must always try to go in the direction of the wood grain.

2. Hand sanding a curved varnished piece using sandpaper and a wood block.

3. The electric belt sander is used to sand large surfaces.

4. Orbital sander smoothing a varnished surface. The white dust is typical of the varnish.

5. A cabinetmaker can finish shaping an object of any form with a half-round rasp.

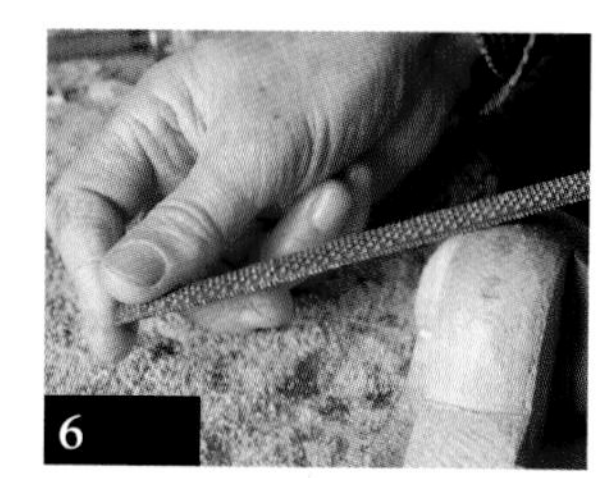

6. The rasp as well as the file must be held at the end opposite the handle.

7. Concave shapes can be filed with a cylindrical file.

8. When using a scraper, the tool must be held with both hands, flexing it slightly, and scraping the surface of the wood until shavings are seen.

FINISHING

Finishing the surface of the wood is the last task performed on any woodworking job. Nowadays, finishing is considered very important because it accomplishes two functions: it protects the wood from outside aggressions and it embellishes the surface.

Treatment with dyes and paint varnishes keeps dust and grime from penetrating the pores of the wood, and prevents the wood from moving as a result of changes in temperature. Besides protecting the wood, these products enhance the beauty of the furniture.

To achieve a proper finish, a cabinetmaker must very closely follow the process explained here.

First, any small imperfections that the wood may have should be filled with a commercial filler, which is easy to apply. It is also necessary to smooth the wood thoroughly before applying any treatment to the surface, because this is the basis of the finish.

Light or semidark woods may be stained with special pigments, which are dissolved in water or alcohol and then used to color the wood.

After the staining, the piece can be varnished, which besides making it beautiful also provides better protection against the outside elements.

The next phase of the finishing process is the sanding and buffing of the varnished surface to remove the imperfections that are produced when the varnish dries; buffing also removes the scratches left by the sandpaper.

Finally, wax is applied and buffed with cheesecloth or a cotton cloth to give the furniture shine.

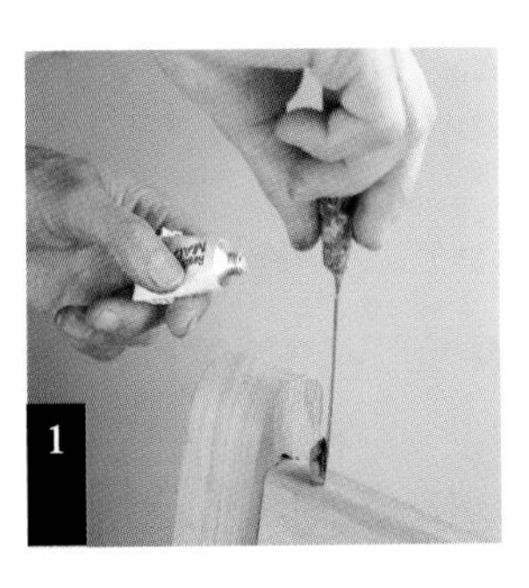

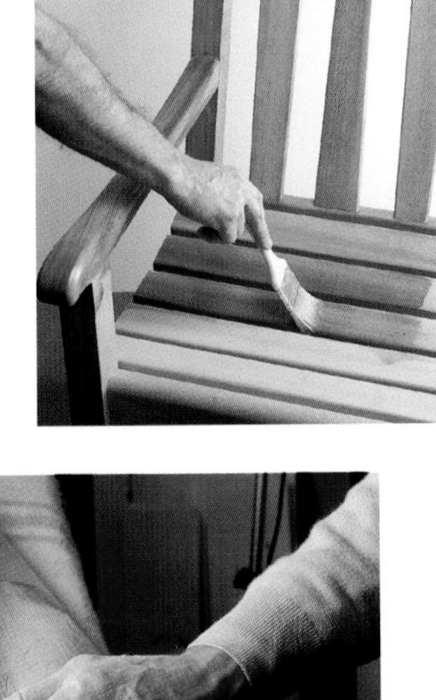

1. One of the first tasks involved in the finishing process is hiding small imperfections or gaps between the joints of the wood, which is done by applying fillers.

2. Staining a piece of wood, in this case cherry, with a mahogany color dye. A brush is used for this task.

3. Applying varnish to the same piece of wood with cotton strands.

4. Applying varnish with a wide brush.

5. Using steel wool to buff a surface that has previously been sanded and varnished.

6. Final application of wax with cotton strands over a buffed surface.

GIRAFFE

The complexity of certain projects resides not in their size, but in the meticulous work that the pieces require to achieve a good finished product. This is the case in the following project, which consists of making a decorative object, in the shape of a giraffe, out of cherry, mountain ash, and walnut wood.

Notice that some power tools have been used, a band saw, for example, as well as hand tools such as gouges and rasps.

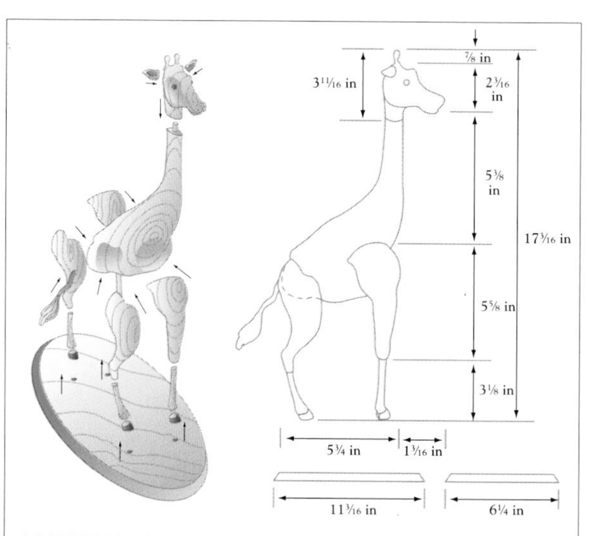

MATERIALS and MEASUREMENTS

Cherry wood for the body: 12 5/8 × 7 7/8 × 2 3/8 inches
Cherry wood for the head: 4 × 4 × 2 3/8 inches and the upper legs 23 5/8 × 2 3/4 × 1 9/16 inches
Mountain ash for the legs: 15 3/4 × 1 × 1 inches
Walnut for the ears, hooves, and tail: 10 × 1 3/16 × 1 3/16 inches
Ebony for the eyes: dowels 3/16 × 2 inches long
Embero for the stand: 11 13/16 × 7 3/32 × 1 inches

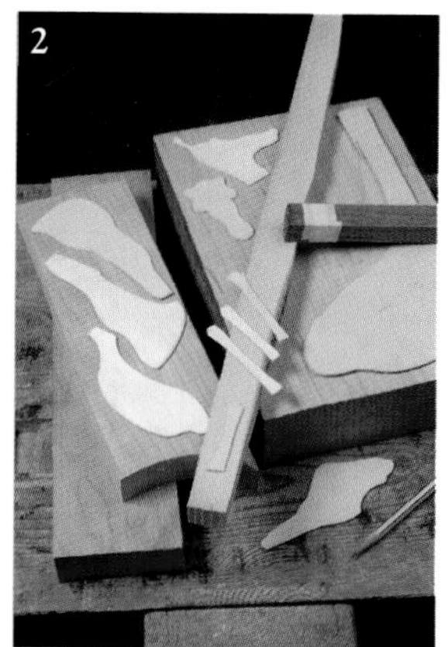

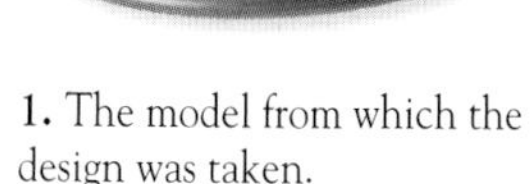

1. The model from which the design was taken.

2. To begin the project, drawings and patterns are made of the giraffe's body and legs. Then, the parts are traced on different pieces of cherry wood.

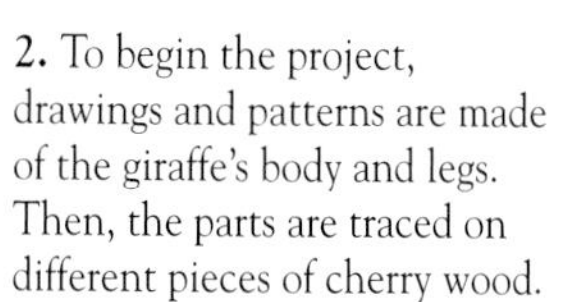

3. Next, with the help of a band saw, the pieces for the body and the top part of the legs of the giraffe are cut.

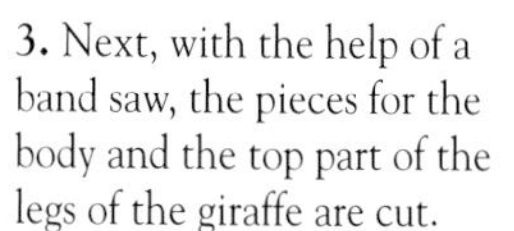

4. It is necessary to cut the pieces from two sides. For the second cut, the wood must be set on its side on the band saw table.

5. The next step is to cut out the front part of the giraffe's face, which is also done on the band saw.

6. The piece that has just been cut out is then held with adhesive tape. The pattern of the profile of the giraffe's head is placed on the side of the wood block and then marked.

7. Once all the cuts of the different profiles have been made, the cabinetmaker is left with a roughly shaped head for the giraffe.

8. Next, this piece is attached to the bench vise, where the head is shaped with different types of gouges.

9. The holes for the eyes are made with a drill, where round pieces of a darker wood will later be inserted.

10. Using a table saw, two incisions are made in the body of the giraffe, where the hind legs will be inserted. It must be noted that these cuts are dangerous to make because it is not possible to rest the whole piece of wood on the surface of the table saw.

11. Then, the body of the giraffe is attached to the workbench with a clamp. The joints are made with a gouge in order for the front legs to fit perfectly.

12. To form the neck, the piece is attached to the workbench and shaped with a rasp until a more or less cylindrical form has been achieved.

13. While being held with a bench vise, the legs are also shaped with a rasp.

14. When the piece has small curved forms, a round file must be used.

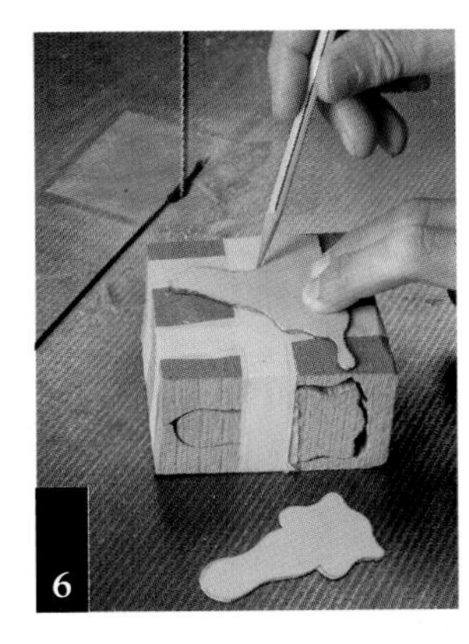
6

7

8

9

10

11

12

13

14

15. To attach all the legs to the giraffe's body, small holes are made with a drill where both pieces will be joined together with a nail.

16. Next, another hole will be made on the bottom of the leg, where the lower leg piece will be attached.

17. To make the lower legs, the contours are traced from the patterns onto mountain ash wood, and then they are cut out with a band saw. The cuts separating the pieces are made with a tenon saw.

18. After that, the lower legs are shaped and smoothed using a round file.

19. To carve the giraffe's ears, the design is first marked on the wood. Then the hollow area is carved out, cutting around the sides of the ears until finally separating them from the excess wood.

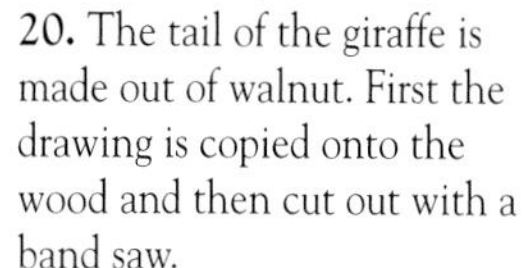

20. The tail of the giraffe is made out of walnut. First the drawing is copied onto the wood and then cut out with a band saw.

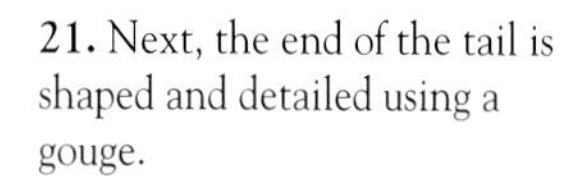

21. Next, the end of the tail is shaped and detailed using a gouge.

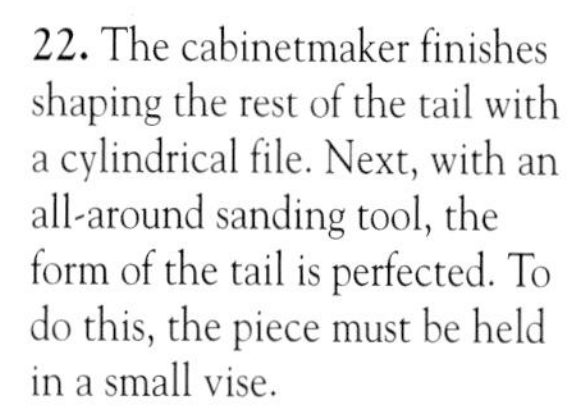

22. The cabinetmaker finishes shaping the rest of the tail with a cylindrical file. Next, with an all-around sanding tool, the form of the tail is perfected. To do this, the piece must be held in a small vise.

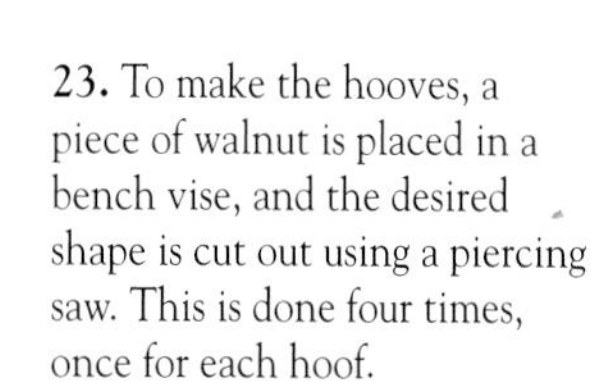

23. To make the hooves, a piece of walnut is placed in a bench vise, and the desired shape is cut out using a piercing saw. This is done four times, once for each hoof.

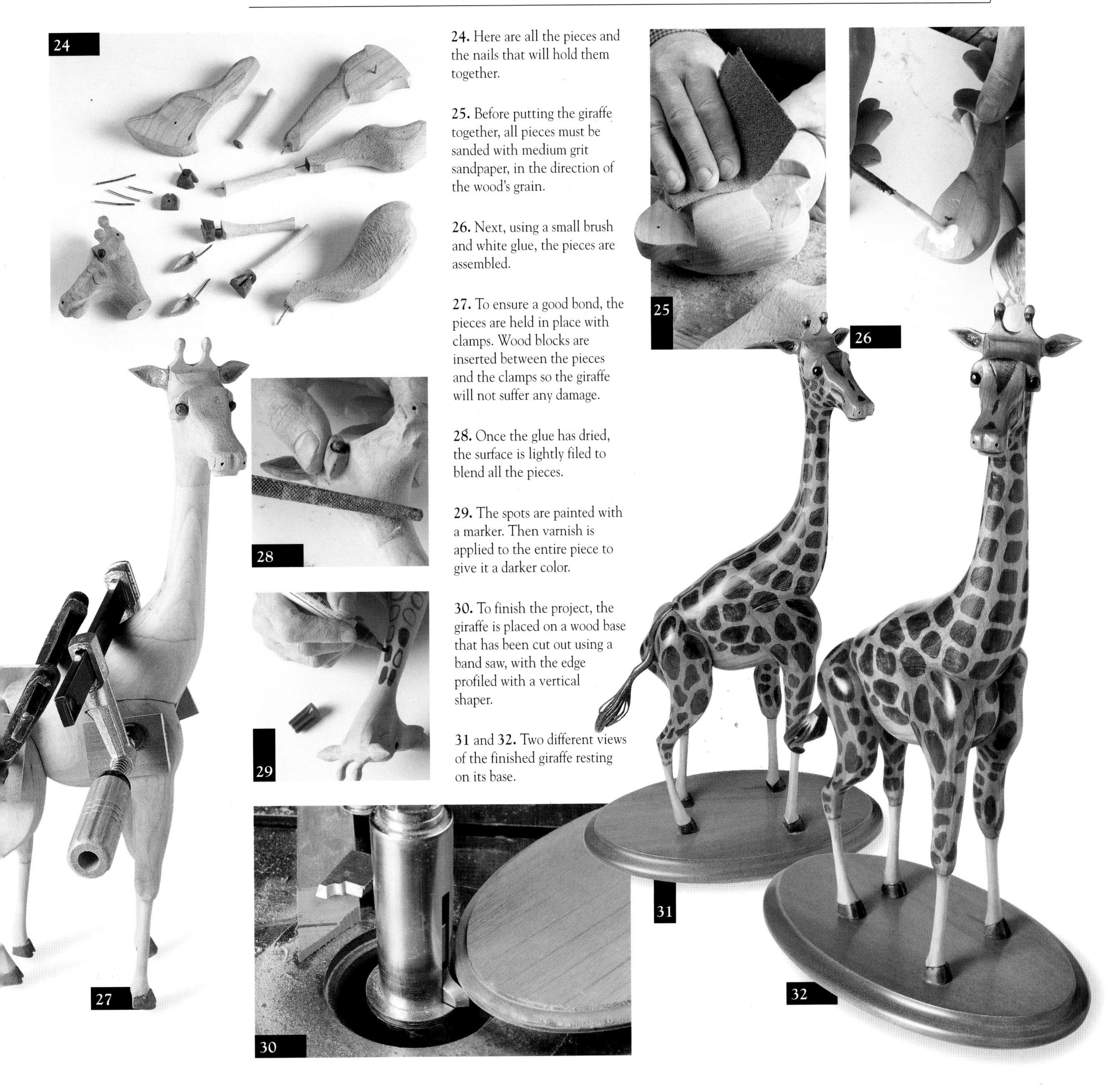

24. Here are all the pieces and the nails that will hold them together.

25. Before putting the giraffe together, all pieces must be sanded with medium grit sandpaper, in the direction of the wood's grain.

26. Next, using a small brush and white glue, the pieces are assembled.

27. To ensure a good bond, the pieces are held in place with clamps. Wood blocks are inserted between the pieces and the clamps so the giraffe will not suffer any damage.

28. Once the glue has dried, the surface is lightly filed to blend all the pieces.

29. The spots are painted with a marker. Then varnish is applied to the entire piece to give it a darker color.

30. To finish the project, the giraffe is placed on a wood base that has been cut out using a band saw, with the edge profiled with a vertical shaper.

31 and 32. Two different views of the finished giraffe resting on its base.

GARDEN CHAIR

The following project is a garden chair made of teak. Although power tools have been used to make the project easier, the chair can be made with simpler tools. The tasks that stand out in this project are the methods of making patterns, the marking, the joining, and the finishing. The woodworker, as usual, must begin the work with a design and then follow it through as the piece of furniture is created.

MATERIALS and MEASUREMENTS

Teak for:

- **2 rear legs: $38\frac{7}{8} \times 7\frac{3}{32} \times 2$ inches**
- **2 front legs: $51\frac{3}{16} \times 2\frac{5}{32} \times 2$ inches**
- **1 rear seat rail: $26\frac{7}{8} \times 3\frac{15}{16} \times 1\frac{1}{2}$ inches**
- **1 front seat rail: $26\frac{7}{8} \times 3\frac{5}{32} \times 1\frac{1}{2}$ inches**
- **2 side seat rails: $78 \times 3 \times 1\frac{1}{2}$ inches**
- **2 side stretcher rails: $78 \times 2 \times 1\frac{1}{4}$ inches**
- **2 arm rests: $47\frac{1}{4} \times 2 \times 2$ inches**
- **1 crest rail: $26\frac{7}{8} \times 3 \times 1\frac{1}{4}$ inches**
- **5 seat slats: $133\frac{7}{8} \times 2\frac{3}{4} \times 1\frac{1}{4}$ inches**
- **5 back slats: $86\frac{5}{8} \times 3 \times \frac{3}{4}$ inches**
- **2 corner braces: $11\frac{13}{16} \times 3\frac{5}{32} \times 1\frac{1}{2}$ inches**

Measurements of the wood before planing.

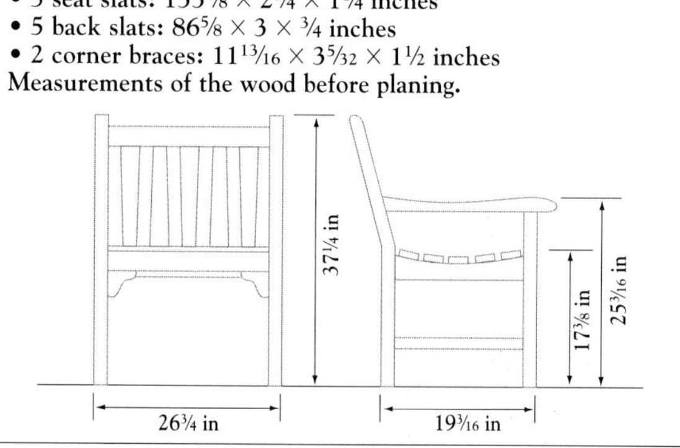

1. A full-scale drawing of the design on a sheet of plywood.
2. The different pieces are traced on tracing paper.
3. The tracing paper is placed on a sheet of plywood and the lines are retraced as if it were carbon paper.
4. Using a jigsaw to cut out the different pieces that will be used as patterns.
5. The process is repeated until all of the patterns have been created.

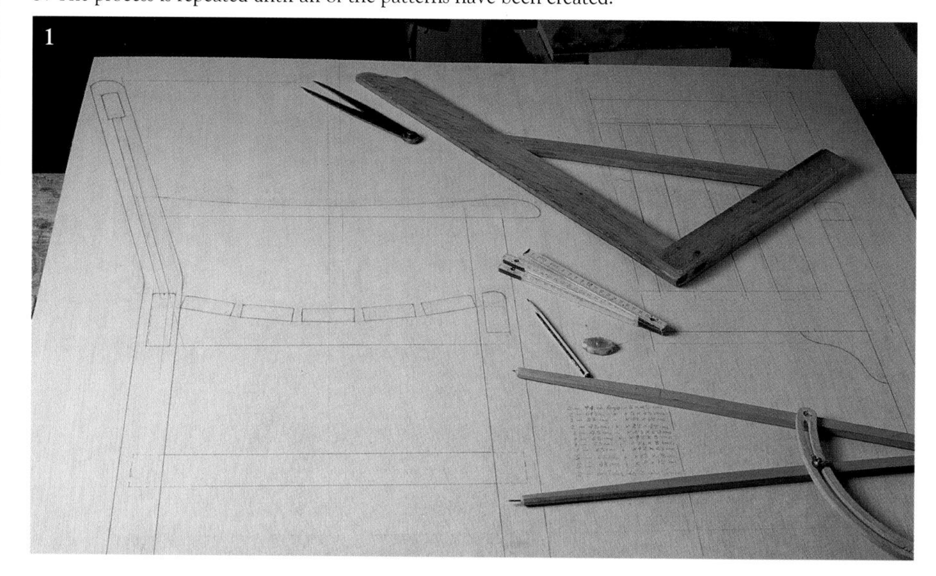
1

2

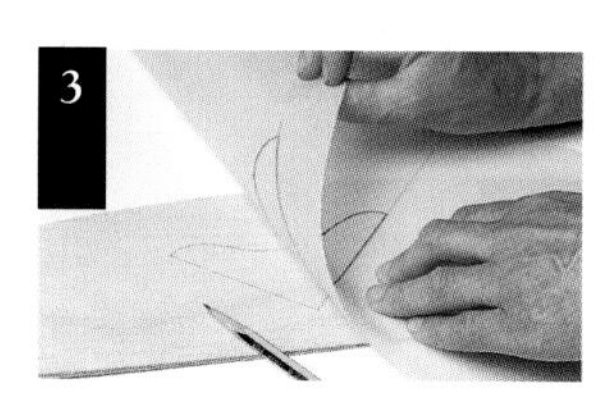
3

4

5

6. Now, the patterns can be placed on the teak, trying to use the wood as efficiently as possible.

7. Then, the wood boards are cut lengthwise with a band saw.

8. The faces and edges are smoothed using an electric jointer.

9. The faces of the parts are made parallel with the thickness planer.

10. The different pieces to be made are drawn, tracing the patterns on the planed wood.

11. All the different parts are cut out using the band saw. In this case, the back legs of the chair are being cut.

12. Even if the band saw blade is wide, it is easy to follow the curved lines on the back legs.

13. All the parts of the chair will be cut out following the same process. Here, the side stretcher rail is being cut out.

14. Patterns and cut parts ready for the chair's back.

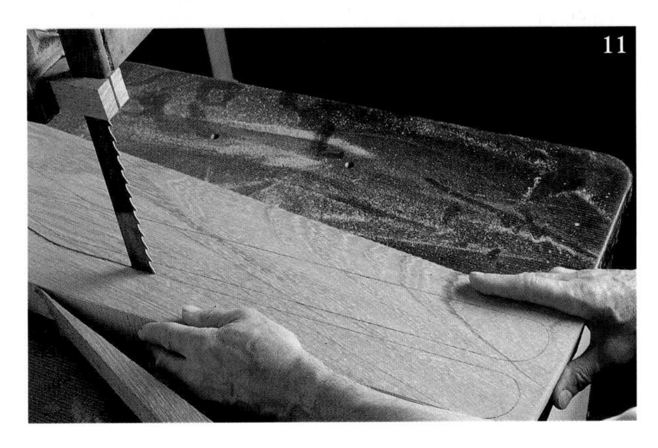

15. A pattern and a part for an armrest.

16. The layout of the mortises for the slats on the chair's back and locating them on the pieces.

17. Planing of the inside of the legs must be done manually with a hand plane.

18. Next, the locations of the parts and the mortises for the joints are marked.

19. The mortises are made with the help of a drill press.

20. To make mortises that are not perpendicular to one of the faces of the part, the woodworker makes jigs to hold the parts at an angle while they are being drilled.

21. The widths of the tenons that will fit into the mortises are measured with a marking gauge.

22. The tenons are cut on a vertical shaper adapted with a horizontal blade.

23. The excess wood is cut away from the tenons with the backsaw.

24. The edges of the tenons are rounded with the rasp so they will fit into the mortise.

25. The edges of the armrest are molded on a vertical shaper.

26. With the same vertical shaper, the rounded edges of the seat rails are molded.

27. Notice that the joints cross here, which requires making adjustments to the tenons.

28. Using a handheld power drill, holes are made in the top part of the side seat rails to insert the dowels.

29. More holes are drilled with the same tool so that the seat rails can be joined with the slats of the seat.

30. Before proceeding with the gluing, the chair must be assembled to make sure that all pieces fit together.

31. All the pieces are sanded on both sides and on the flat edges, with an electric belt sander or by hand.

32. The curved parts are sanded using a belt sander that has been clamped in an inverted position.

33. It is preferable to smooth the corners manually. Sandpaper will be used for this task.

34. When the sanding is finished, the gluing begins. On the side seat rails, this is done while also adjusting the length of the dowels.

35. The next step is to glue the pieces that form one side of the chair and to hold them together with clamps.

36. Gluing the corner brace to the front seat rail with dowels.

37. Gluing the chair back. Notice how the angled mortise creates a slanted back.

38. A view of the various parts that will form the chair.

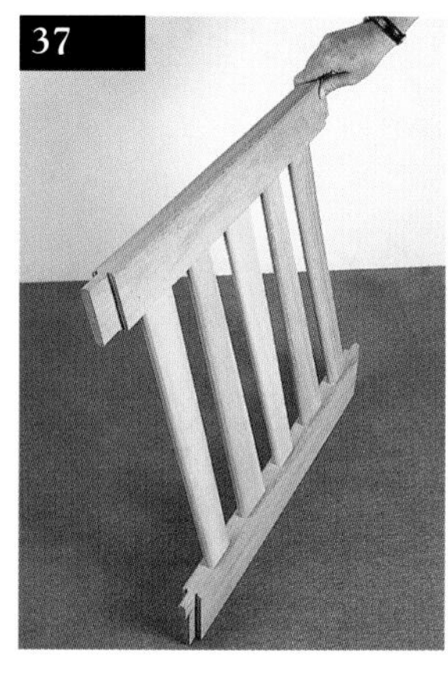

39. Gluing the front seat rail and the remaining pieces. Notice that the corner brace should have been attached already.

40. Holding the entire piece of furniture together with clamps.

41. When the glue is dry, the small imperfections are covered with filler of the same color as the wood.

42. The final sanding is done manually.

43. For the final finish, a special exterior sealant is applied with a brush.

44. After the varnish is sanded, the chair is cleaned.

45. Garden chair project completed.

MULTIPURPOSE BOX

There are some projects where the reduced dimensions of the object chosen determine the level of difficulty. The following project involves building a multipurpose box.

Cedar wood is used for the structure of the box; mahogany and erable veneer for the drawers and lid; teak for the moldings; and American walnut for the edges.

MATERIALS and MEASUREMENTS

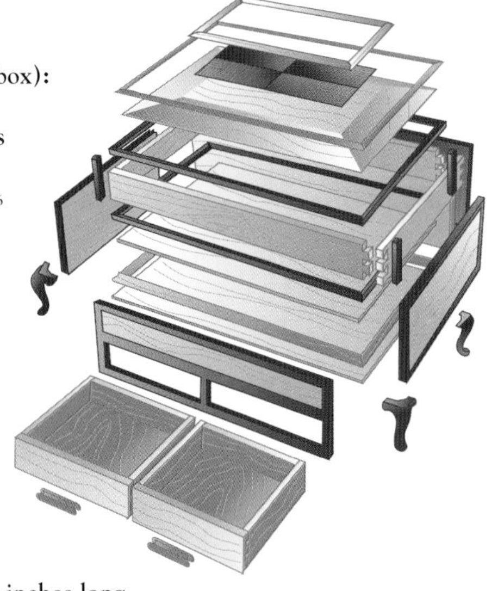

Cedar wood for:
- 2 structures (back and sides of the box): $23\frac{7}{8} \times 2\frac{3}{8} \times \frac{9}{32}$ inches
- 1 front piece: $9\frac{2}{8} \times 1\frac{1}{8} \times \frac{9}{32}$ inches
- 1 bottom: $10\frac{1}{8} \times 6\frac{15}{16} \times \frac{1}{4}$ inches
- 1 drawer separator: $6\frac{5}{8} \times 1\frac{9}{16} \times \frac{3}{16}$ inches

Cedar wood with erable veneer for:
- 1 front piece for a drawer: $11\frac{13}{16} \times 1\frac{3}{8} \times \frac{1}{2}$ inches
- 1 side for drawers: $28 \times 1\frac{3}{8} \times \frac{9}{32}$ inches
- 1 rear side for drawers: $11\frac{13}{16} \times 1 \times \frac{3}{16}$ inches

Mahogany veneer for:
- 4 combined veneer pieces for the lid: $3\frac{15}{16} \times 2$ inches

Walnut wood for:
- Borders: $\frac{3}{8} \times \frac{3}{8} \times \frac{3}{32}$ inches—$15\frac{3}{4}$ inches long
- Covers for around the box: $\frac{1}{4} \times \frac{3}{32}$ inches—$72\frac{7}{8}$ inches long
- Box top cover: $\frac{7}{16} \times \frac{3}{32}$ inches—$36\frac{5}{8}$ inches long

Teak for:
- Lower molding of the box: $\frac{15}{16} \times \frac{5}{8}$ inches—$43\frac{5}{16}$ inches long
- Molding for the edge of the lid: $\frac{9}{16} \times \frac{7}{16}$ inches—$43\frac{5}{16}$ inches long
- Molding for the central piece of the lid: $\frac{5}{16} \times \frac{5}{32}$ inches—$25\frac{5}{8}$ inches long

Abebay wood for:
- 4 legs: $11\frac{13}{16} \times 1\frac{5}{8} \times 1\frac{5}{8}$ inches
- 2 pulls: $6 \times \frac{7}{16} \times \frac{5}{16}$ inches

2 brass hinges $\frac{5}{8} \times 1\frac{5}{8}$ inches with their respective brass screws.
Exact width and thickness measurements.

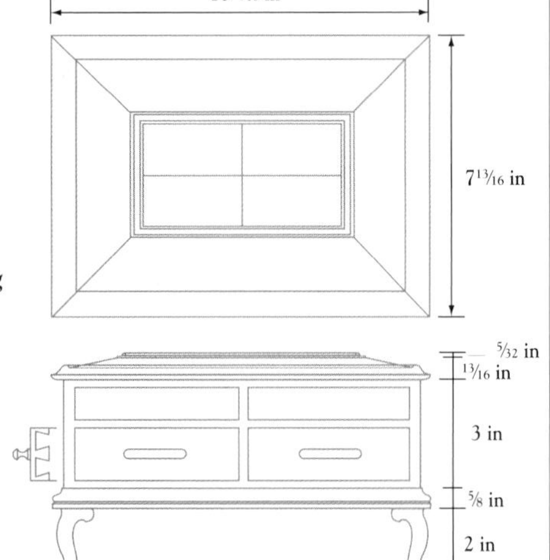

1. First, the design of the project should be laid out on paper. Then, the large and small strips of wood and all of the other pieces of wood needed for the job are prepared.

2. The strips of wood are shaped with a vertical shaper. To do this, the piece should rest on the tabletop of the machine and against one side guide. Because the blade of the machine is exposed, caution should be used.

3. A specific cutting blade will be used for each type of molding.

4. The same vertical shaper will be used to make the grooves and the necessary adjustments for fitting together the different cedar pieces that make up the structure of the box.

5. The interior faces of the box are sanded while resting them on a workbench. Medium grit sandpaper is used for this task.

6. White glue is spread on the wood pieces. A small brush is recommended to avoid staining the wood.

7. The box is assembled, aligning the pieces carefully and holding them in place with regular clamps or spring clamps.

8. The spindle shaper must be used to bevel the surface of the box lid. Once the angle has been set, the four bevels are formed.

9. Next, the veneers that will cover the box are cut using a shear. The light-colored ones are made of erable wood and the dark ones of mahogany.

10. The four sheets of mahogany are joined together with masking tape, forming designs with the combination of their grain. The adhesive tape is placed on the outside of the sheets.

11. Contact cement is applied to the two surfaces that are to be bonded (veneer and box top). Then they are put in place and pressure is applied to the entire surface.

12. The four sheets that will go on the beveled areas of the lid must be aligned before applying the contact cement and bonding them.

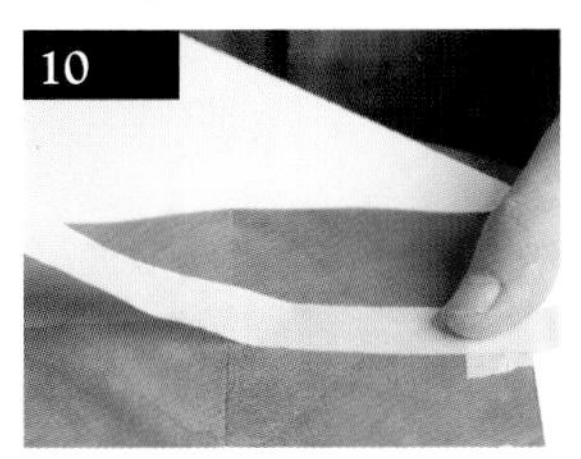

13. The veneer is sanded with medium grit sandpaper. This is done vigorously, making sure the wood is perfectly clean.

14. Next, the molding for the lid will be cut at a 45-degree angle. To carry out this task, a tenon saw and a miter guide are used.

15. The bottom moldings are attached to the box with a tongue-and-groove. Molding is also attached where the two veneers meet.

16. After applying white glue, the bottom moldings are aligned and held firmly in place with clamps.

17. The same procedure is followed for attaching the top moldings.

18. To apply pressure to the top moldings, a piece of board and a weight of about 2 lbs. (1 kg) are used.

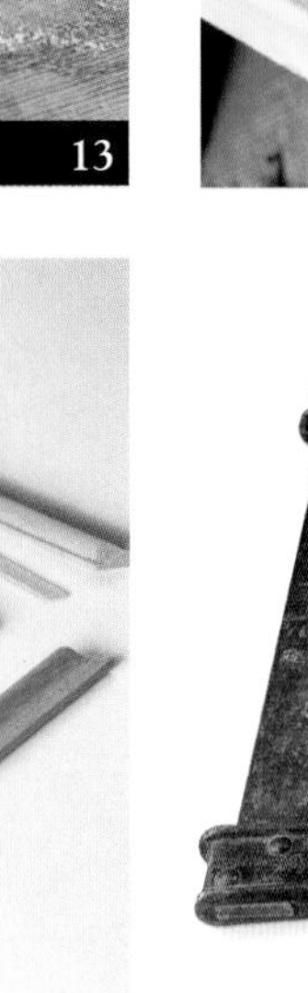

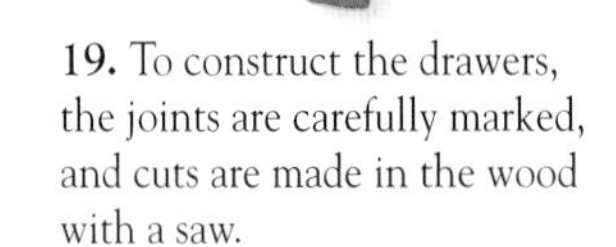

19. To construct the drawers, the joints are carefully marked, and cuts are made in the wood with a saw.

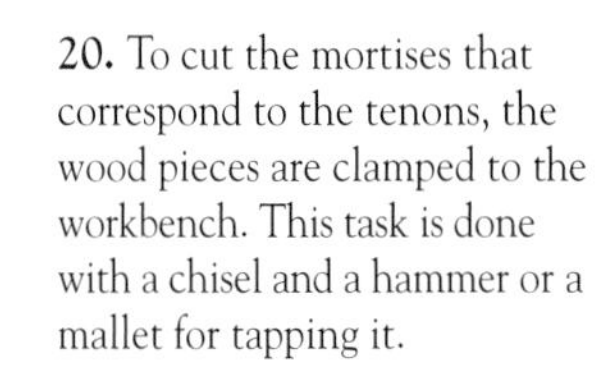

20. To cut the mortises that correspond to the tenons, the wood pieces are clamped to the workbench. This task is done with a chisel and a hammer or a mallet for tapping it.

21

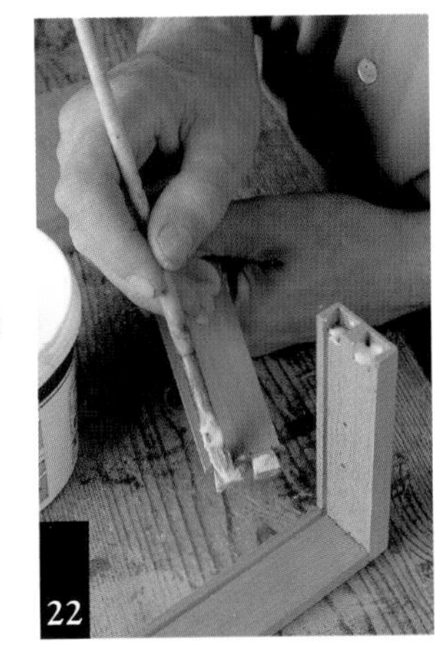
22

23

21. Notice that the drawer is made up of the front and side pieces, the back piece, and the bottom.

22. All the pieces are bonded with white glue. The grooves on the wood pieces are for holding the drawer bottom. The two holes on the front piece will be used to attach the drawer pull.

23. The excess wood is removed from the frame of the box with a carpenter's plane.

24. To cover the box with veneer, contact cement is spread over the two surfaces that need to be bonded. A spatula can be used for this task.

25. When the glue feels dry to the touch, both pieces can be put together. In this case, erable wood veneer is used, and it is pressed with a hammer designed for this task.

26. The excess veneer is removed with a fine file. To perform the task, attach the box to the workbench.

27. Before the corners are glued in place, all the sides of the box should be sanded with medium grit sandpaper.

28. Now, the corners can be cut out of American walnut and glued with white glue. They are attached to the box and held in place with spring clamps.

27

25

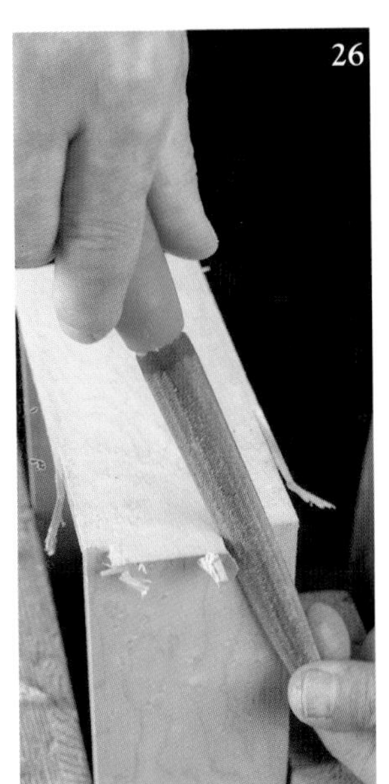
26

28

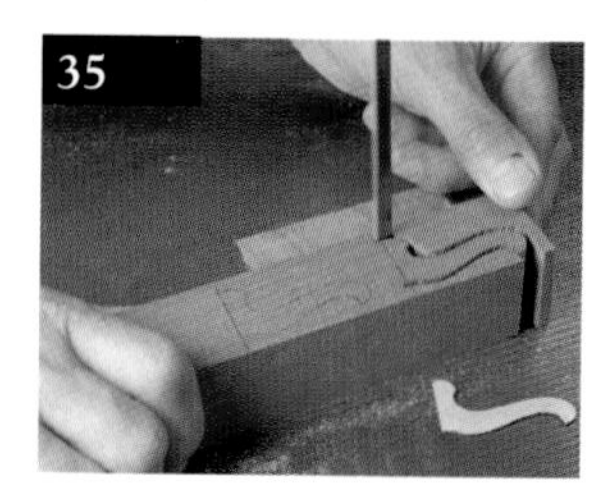

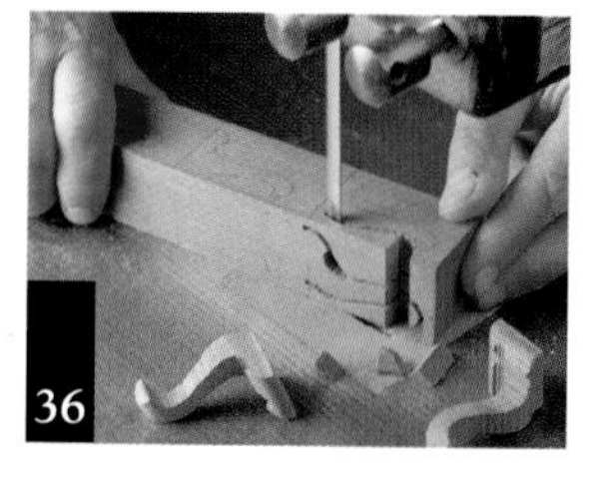

29. In the same way, the wood strips can be attached to the top edges of the box.

30. The wood strips and corner pieces can be touched up with a file.

31. Then, the pieces that have been glued on are sanded. The sanding should be done following the direction of the grain of the wood.

32. The molding pieces for the bottom edge of the box are then cut with a 45-degree miter and glued together. Picture frame clamps can be used to hold them.

33. Now the molding can be glued to the box. The glue is first applied to both pieces and then the box is placed on the molding.

34. To achieve a good bond, the box is placed between two boards and pressure is applied with clamps.

35. Abebay wood is used to make the feet. They are shaped with a band saw, making cuts on one side of the wood.

36. Following the same procedure, the feet are cut on the other side of the wood block.

37. Shaping is completed using a round file. The leg has been attached to the workbench using two pieces of wood.

38. The legs are attached to the box with white glue.

39. To apply pressure to them and to the box, two screws are inserted into the holes that have been previously drilled in the wood.

40. The wood on the top edge of the box is removed to insert the hinges. To do this a chisel is used, first making some small cuts and then removing the excess wood.

41. Once the hinges have been set in place, holes are drilled and the screws inserted.

42. The drawer pulls are also attached with screws.

43. The final finish is applied by varnishing the box. To do this, it is a good idea to disassemble the parts of the box that are not glued by removing all of the hardware.

44. The completed multi-purpose box.

SERVING CART

The following exercise shows how to make a serving cart in teak. The cart is made up of two trays, one above and one below; the bottom one has a rack for holding bottles. Two front wheels allow the piece to be pushed easily from one place to another. The back end is supported by two slanted legs, which provide stability to the entire piece.

To make this cart, the woodworker will need the help of a wood turner for the preparation of the various cylindrical pieces, such as the wheel spokes, the handle of the cart, and some dowels.

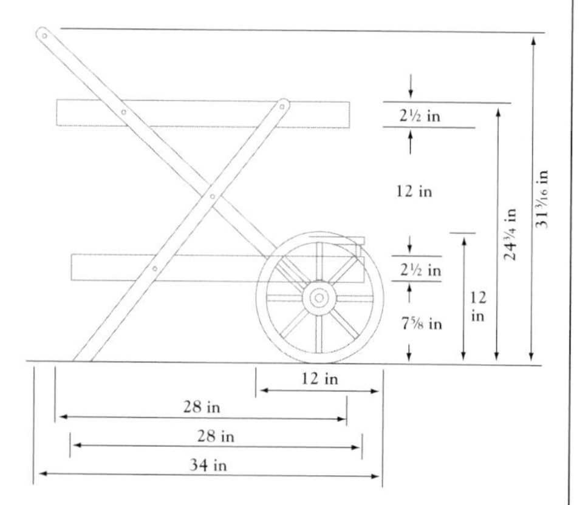

MATERIALS and MEASUREMENTS
Teak (iroco) for:

- **2 front legs: $37\frac{1}{2} \times 1\frac{3}{8} \times 1\frac{3}{16}$ inches**
- **2 rear legs: $31\frac{1}{2} \times 1\frac{3}{8} \times 1\frac{3}{16}$ inches**
- **4 frame pieces for the trays: $27\frac{7}{16} \times 2\frac{3}{8} \times \frac{11}{16}$ inches**
- **4 frame pieces for the trays: $17\frac{3}{4} \times 2\frac{3}{8} \times \frac{11}{16}$ inches**
- **26 slats for tray bottoms: $17\frac{1}{8} \times 2 \times \frac{9}{32}$ inches**
- **2 wooden wheels: $86\frac{5}{8} \times 4 \times 1$ inches**
- **16 round dowels $\frac{1}{2}$ inch diameter and 4 inches long**
- **1 turned handle: $19 \times 1\frac{3}{16} \times 1\frac{3}{16}$ inches**
- **1 board for bottle holder: $17\frac{3}{4} \times 5\frac{1}{8} \times \frac{11}{16}$ inches**

Threaded metal studs of $\frac{5}{16}$ inches diameter and 4 brass cap nuts or acorn nuts.
Threaded metal studs of $\frac{3}{16}$ inches diameter and 18 brass cap nuts or acorn nuts.

1. After the working drawing is done, measurements are marked on the two wood boards for the different pieces needed to make the cart.

2. Next, all the required pieces are cut with a band saw.

3. The pieces are smoothed on a plane, pressing the wood firmly against the surface of the machine.

4. The pieces are put through the thickness planer. The woodworker uses a board to apply more pressure on the wood, which offers some resistance when it is inserted in the machine.

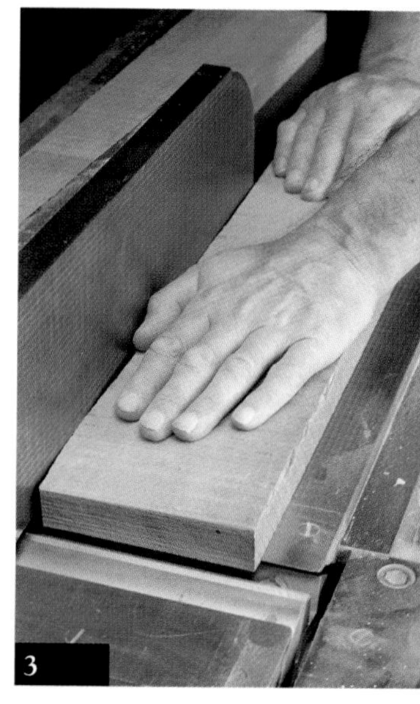

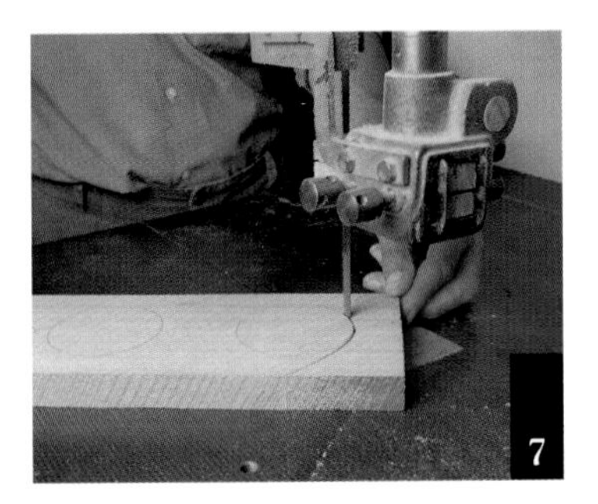

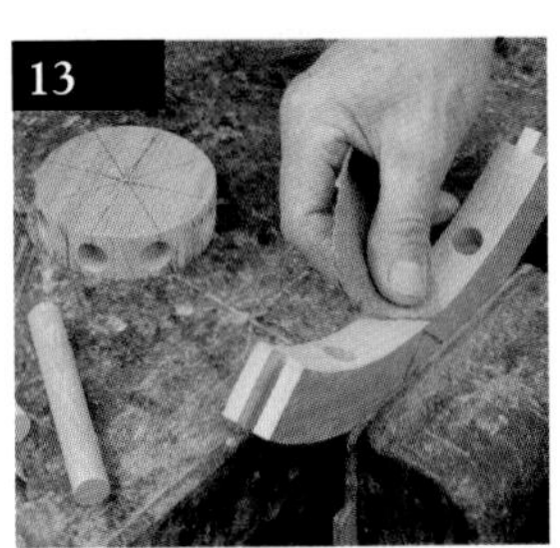

5. The pieces have been cut and planed, and the woodworker is ready to begin making the cart.

6. First, the parts are marked to make the wheels of the cart.

7. The hubs of the wheels are cut out with a band saw.

8. The quarter sections that make up the circumference of the wheels are then cut out.

9. The joining surfaces of the quarter sections of the wheels are cut with a radial arm saw. To make an accurate cut, the piece should be rested on a wood pattern.

10. Using the same wood pattern, each piece is clamped in place in order to drill the holes where the dowels of the wheels will be inserted.

11. The holes in the hub of the wheel are made the same way.

12. Using a table saw that has been adjusted to the proper setting, cuts are made on the ends of the wheel sections to allow the insertion of splines.

13. The inside surfaces of the pieces are sanded. Holding them with the workbench vise makes the job easier.

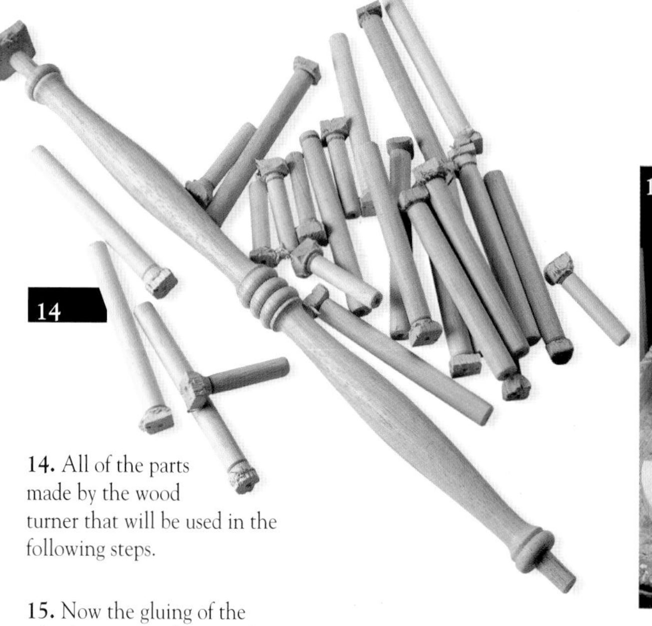

14. All of the parts made by the wood turner that will be used in the following steps.

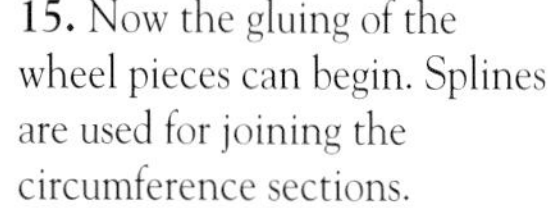

15. Now the gluing of the wheel pieces can begin. Splines are used for joining the circumference sections.

16. To guarantee a good bond, pressure should be applied with a frame clamp for about two hours. The corner pieces have been removed from the clamp.

17. When the gluing is finished, the surface of the wheels is shaped with a rasp. To perform the work more comfortably, the pieces are held in the bench vise.

18. Holes are made in the centers of the wheels with a drill for the axles to pass through.

19. With a vertical shaper, a half-round channel is made on the outside of the wheels.

20. This channel will hold a rubber strip that will make the cart roll easier. Both ends of the rubber strip have been cut so the seam will be perfect.

21. The woodworker begins work on the trays by using a marking gauge to lay out the dovetail joints on one of the side pieces.

22. Next, cuts are made with a tenon saw. For this task, the piece is held in place with the bench vise.

23. The excess wood is removed with a chisel. The use of a wooden mallet is recommended for applying extra force.

24. After the dovetails on one piece are finished, the others are marked with a pencil. Then the joints are cut in the same way as before.

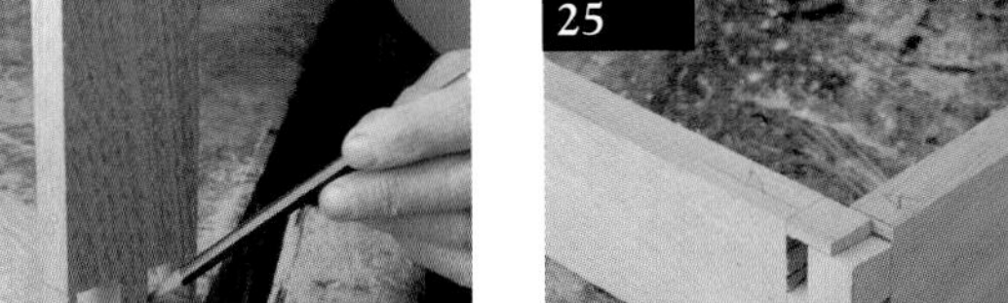

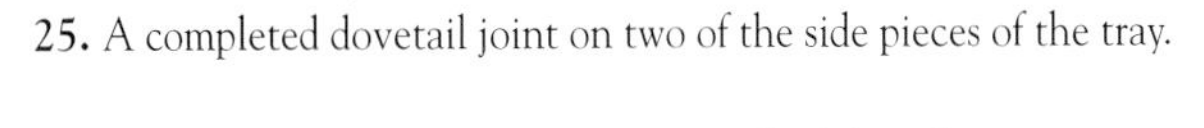

25. A completed dovetail joint on two of the side pieces of the tray.

26. A groove is made with a table saw on all of the side pieces where the slats of the trays will be inserted later.

27. The wood slats that will be used for the bottoms of the trays.

28. A round molded edge is cut on the edges of the slats so that there will be a small space between them when the tray is assembled.

29. The inside surfaces of the frames are smoothed with a belt sander before the trays are assembled and glued. Notice how the wood is held in place with bench dogs.

30. The slats are inserted into the grooves made on the sides of the frame. It is not necessary to glue the slats in place.

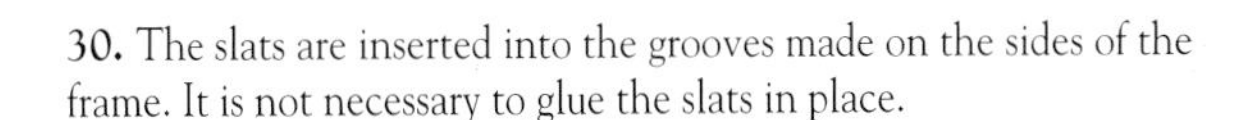

31. Then the dovetail joints are glued. The white glue is applied over the entire surface of the joints with a small brush.

32. To set the side pieces in place, they are tapped with a hammer. A block of wood is placed between the piece and the hammer to avoid damaging the teak.

33. Next, the joints of the side crosspieces are marked. Because the joint is not located at the end of the piece of wood, a sliding bevel is used.

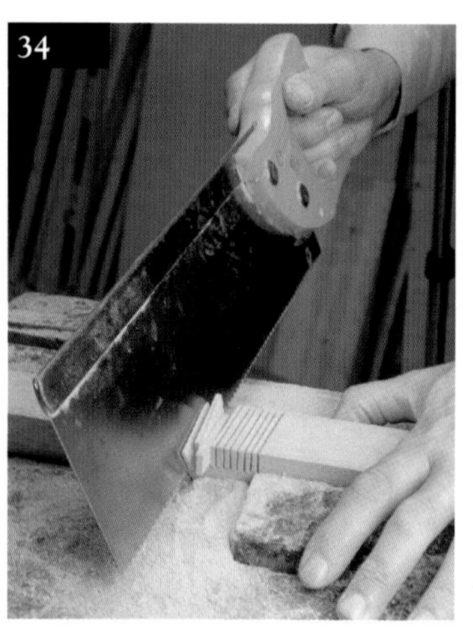

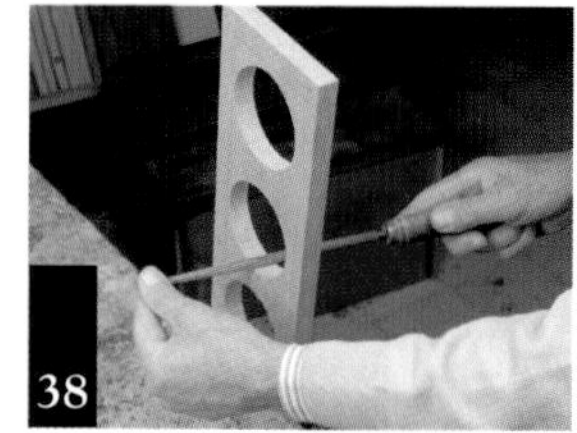

34. Several cuts are made with a tenon saw. By slightly twisting the saw, the excess wood can be broken away.

35. A rasp is used to finish smoothing the joint. This will guarantee that the parts will all fit perfectly.

36. White glue is applied to the joint in the middle of the crosspieces and they are tapped into place with a hammer, using a wood block between the hammer and the wood.

37. To make the bottle holder, the circles are cut out with a jigsaw. Holes should be drilled first in order to insert the jigsaw blade.

38. The piece is held in the workbench and the woodworker finishes shaping the holes with a round file.

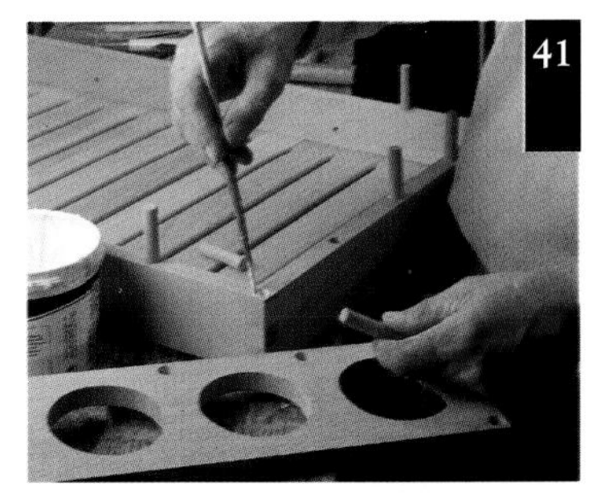

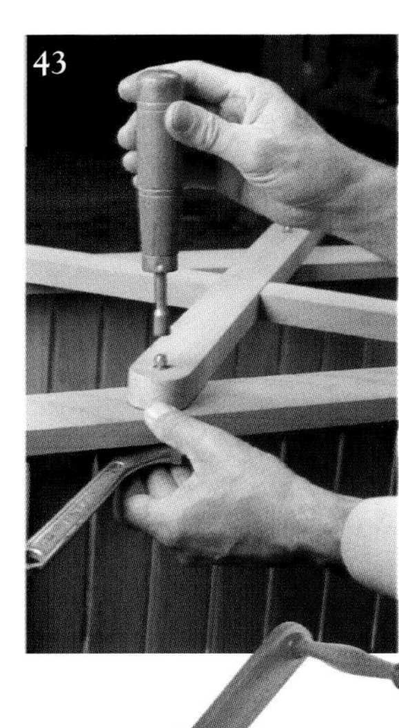

39. The holes to attach the bottle holder to the lower tray are made with a drill press. Notice the dowels that will be used to join the two parts.

40. Then holes are drilled in the frame of the lower tray.

41. Using a small brush, white glue is applied to the holes and to the dowels, which were made of teak by the wood turner.

42. All the pieces are sanded with medium grit sandpaper.

43. Now the cart is ready to be assembled. First, the side crosspieces are attached to the top and bottom trays with threaded screws.

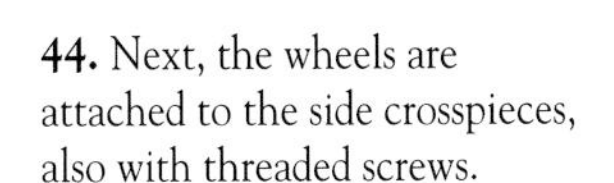

44. Next, the wheels are attached to the side crosspieces, also with threaded screws.

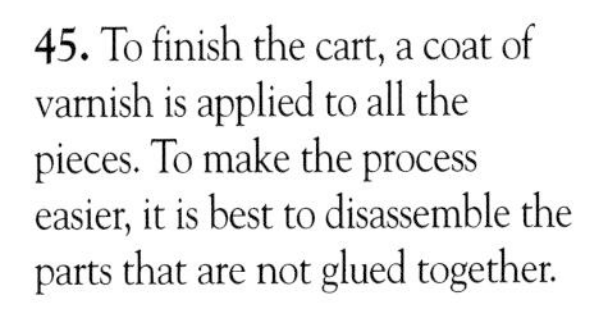

45. To finish the cart, a coat of varnish is applied to all the pieces. To make the process easier, it is best to disassemble the parts that are not glued together.

46. The finished serving cart with the bottle holder on the bottom tray.

ENTRANCE HALL TABLE

The piece of furniture shown here is ideal for an entrance hall. It can be made of cherry wood, and a final finish of varnish and wax, materials that will enhance its beauty, can be applied to it.

The difficulty of this project is in drawing the curved pieces. The joints, on the other hand, are very simple, because they are made with dowels.

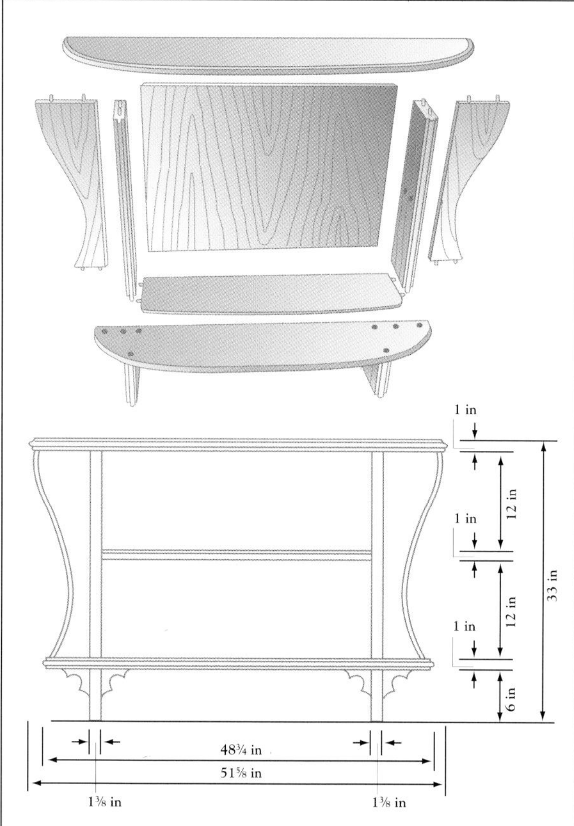

MATERIALS and MEASUREMENTS

Cherry wood for:
- top: 53³⁄₁₆ × 10¼ × 1 inches
- middle shelf: 33½ × 8¼ × 1 inches
- bottom shelf: 49¼ × 9½ × 1 inches
- 2 sides: 25⅝ × 8¼ × 1⅜ inches
- 2 legs: 6¾ × 8¼ × 1⅜ inches
- 2 side curved pieces: 26⅜ × 8¼ × ¾ inches
- braces: 19¾ × 3⁵⁄₃₂ × ¾ inches

1 sheet of cherry faced plywood for the back of the piece: 25¾ × 33¼ × ¼ inches

1. To begin the project, the wood boards are marked before cutting them out and making all the pieces required for the construction of the piece.

2. Cutting is done with a band saw, making sure that the cuts are as straight as possible to make the best use of the wood. The machine has a guide for making such cuts.

3. Once the pieces have been cut, they are passed across the planer. They must be made perfectly smooth, by holding them firmly against the table of the planer as they pass through.

4. Next, the pieces are put through the thickness planer.

5. Planed wood ready to begin the project.

6. The top shelf of the piece must be glued up to make it wider. The additional piece is bonded with white glue and the pieces held in place with clamps.

7. A pattern must be made to use as a guide in tracing the curved pieces. In order to do this, nails are tacked to a board, and a thin strip of wood is passed between them.

8. The outline of the shape is traced with a pencil. The same pattern may be used for two different curved pieces.

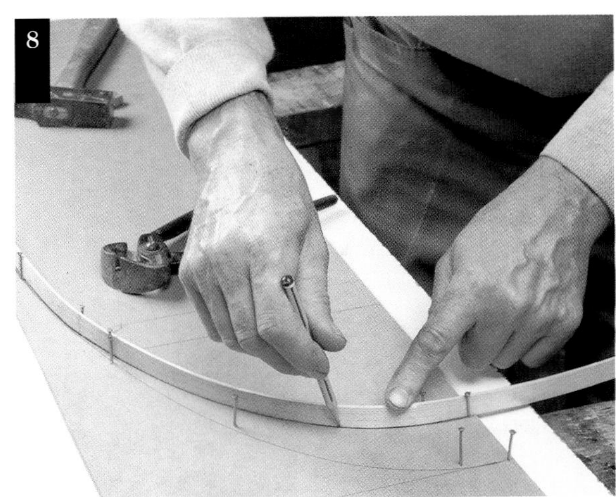

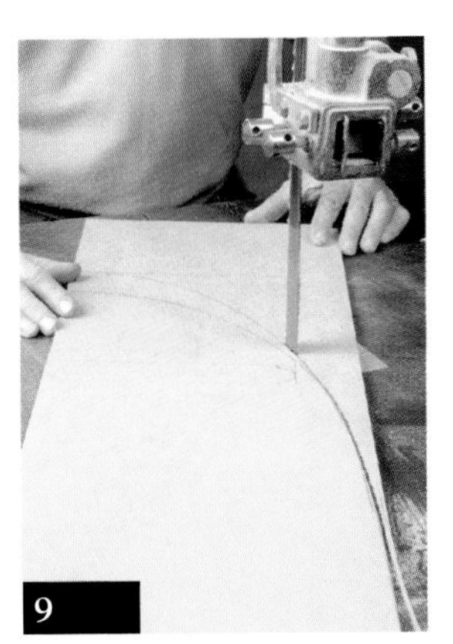

9. The pattern is cut along the largest curve with a band saw.

10. The piece is marked with a pencil after placing the pattern over it.

11. Once the piece has been marked, it is cut out with a band saw. Notice the additional wood that has been glued to the left side.

12. The same procedure is followed to cut out the rest of the furniture parts.

13. The planer can be used to smooth the edges of the pieces. Only wood parts that are large enough to keep the fingers away from the cutting blades should be planed.

14. Concave pieces can be smoothed out with a hand plane. Notice how the wood is firmly held to the workbench.

15. Convex surfaces must be smoothed with rasps and files. At the end of this step, the piece is sanded with sandpaper to make the wood smoother.

16. The edges of the pieces are molded with a vertical shaper. This task must be done carefully to avoid injury.

17. Notice the different moldings and the cutters that have been used to make them.

18. Rabbets are cut on the rear of the top piece, where the back panel of the table will fit into the top.

19. The side panels will be attached to the top with dowel joints. For this purpose, holes are drilled in the top and sides using bits appropriate for this type of wood.

20. Holes made in the top and on one of the side panels of the piece of furniture.

21. A chisel is used to touch up the rabbets on the back side of the tabletop.

22. To make the legs of the piece of furniture, their length is marked with a carpenter's square according to the drawing.

23. To mark the place where the holes should be made, a marking gauge or a carpenter's square is used, together with the measuring tape and a pencil.

24. Once the centers have been marked, the holes are made with an electric drill.

25. Before assembling the table, all of the pieces must be sanded. For correct sanding of the molding, the hand and the sandpaper should be positioned as they are in the picture.

26. For sanding large surfaces, sandpaper is wrapped around a wood block.

27. For large and involved surfaces, an electric sander may also be used to make the task easier.

28. White glue is applied to the dowels with the help of a small brush.

29. The excess wood from the dowels is cut off with a tenon saw, using a piece of wood as a guide.

30. The pieces are shaped and ready to be assembled. They are first put together without glue to check their fit, then they are disassembled for staining and varnishing.

31. The feet are attached to the bottom shelf with dowels.

32. The side boards are placed on the bottom shelf and then the center shelf is attached.

33. The rear side pieces are attached to the shelf and the side boards.

34. Finally, the tabletop and back are attached. After verifying that all the pieces fit perfectly, the woodworker takes them apart.

35. The process of finishing the piece of furniture begins with the selection of the stain, which in this case is mahogany color. The stain is applied with a brush.

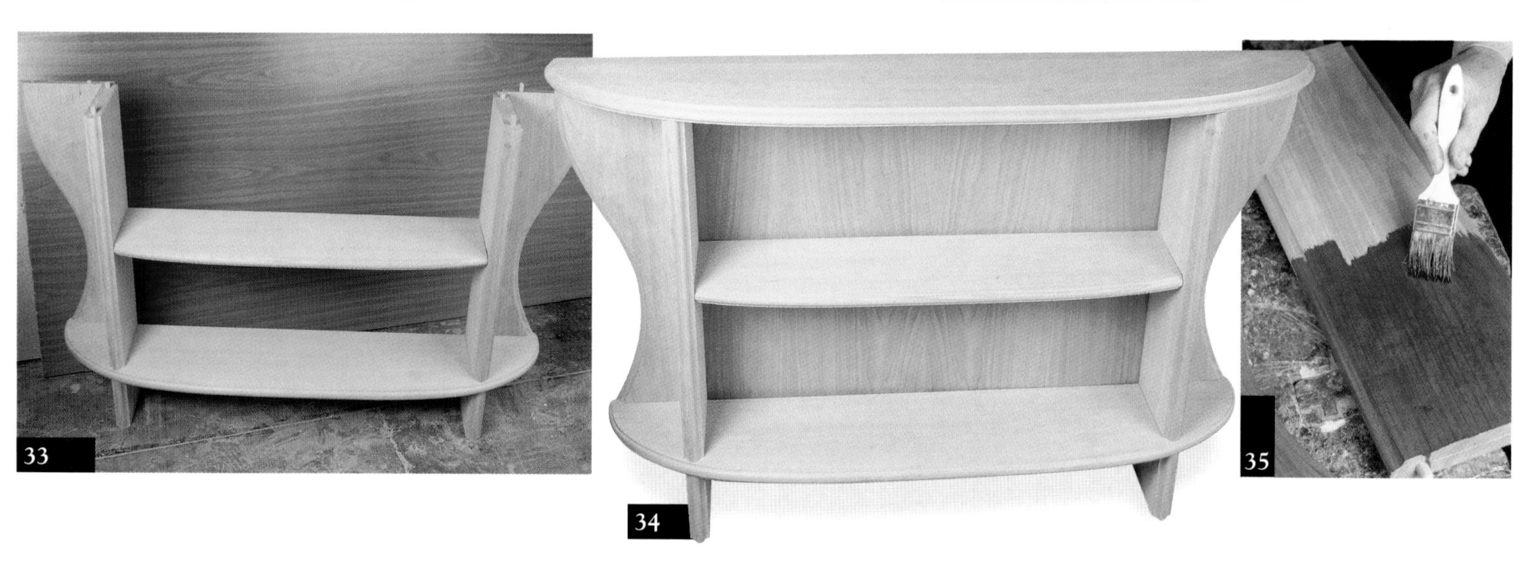

36

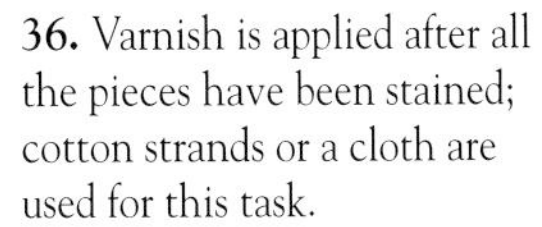

36. Varnish is applied after all the pieces have been stained; cotton strands or a cloth are used for this task.

37. When the varnish is dry, the pieces are smoothed using an orbital sander, and a piece of sandpaper is used to sand the molded edge by hand.

38. The surfaces are rubbed with a steel wool pad.

39. Wax is applied to the furniture parts and buffed with a cloth until the desired gloss is achieved.

40. Then the table is ready to be assembled, beginning with the sides and the shelf.

41. The rear side pieces are attached with screws.

42. Finally, the remaining pieces are glued together with white glue and held in place with clamps.

43. The entrance hall table completely finished.

39

41

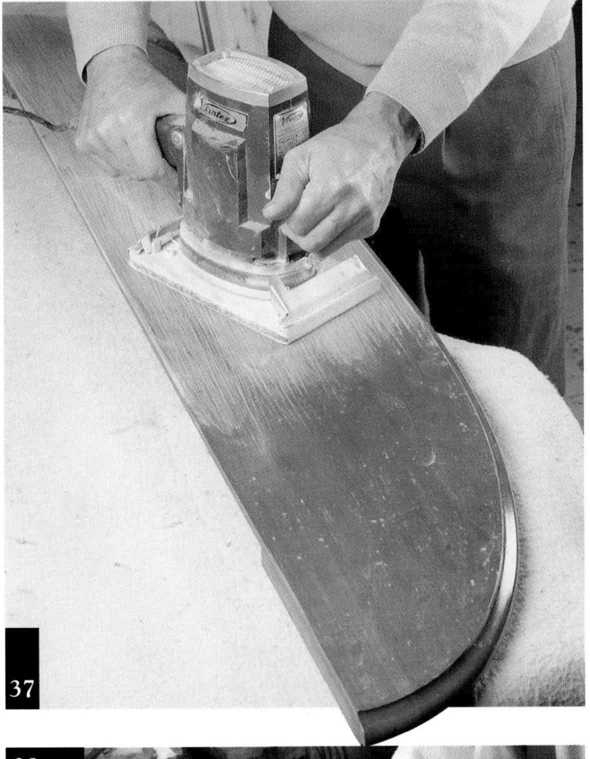

37

40

42

38

43

CORNER DISPLAY CABINET

Making this piece of furniture requires great skill on the part of the woodworker, because of its complexity. It is a corner display cabinet made of two modules with shelves, and its top is finished with a piece that is difficult to make. The wood used for this project is abebay, with the exception of the tops, the side pieces and the door, which are made of veneered plywood boards, and the back panel and the top piece, which are made of plywood board.

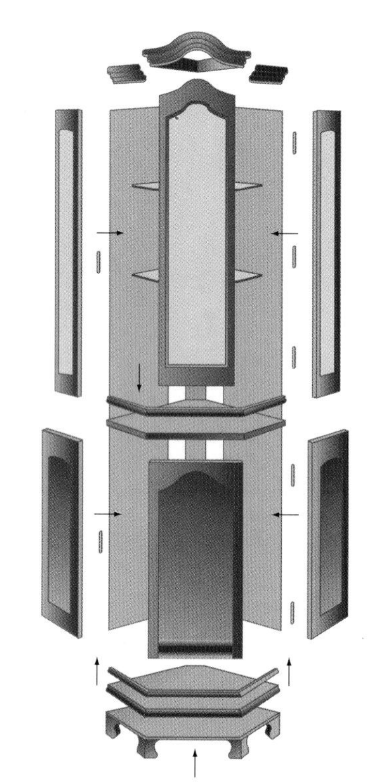

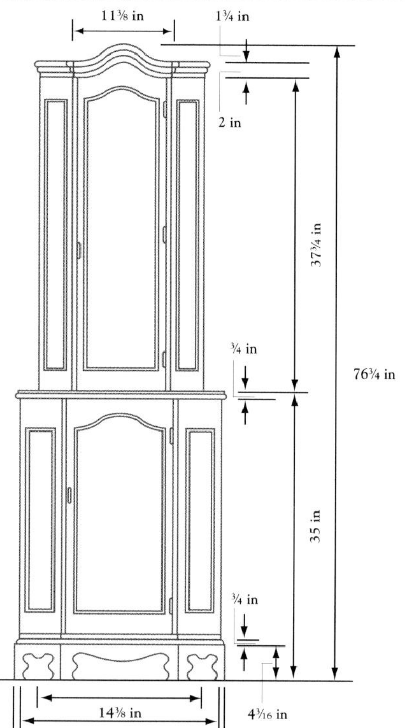

MATERIALS and MEASUREMENTS

Abebay wood for:
- 2 back posts: 70⅞ × 1³⁄₁₆ × 1 inches
- 2 front posts: 70⅞ × 1½ × 1 inches
- 2 doorframes: 70⅞ × 1³⁄₁₆ × 1 inches
- front crosspieces: 72⅞ × 2¾ × 1 inches
- 1 curved door crosspiece: 10⅝ × 4¾ × 1 inches
- 1 wide crosspiece for lower part: 31½ × 3¾ × 1 inches
- top molding: 15¾ × 2 × 1 inches
- curved top moldings: 15¾ × 4 × 1 inches
- middle shelf: 33½ × 4⅛ × 1³⁄₁₆ inches
- bracket base: 33½ × 4¾ × ½ inches
- back side strip: 70⅞ inches

1 plywood board to veneer the curved top of the furniture piece: 31½ × 3 × ⅛ inches
2 abebay boards for the back piece of the furniture: 72⅞ × 17 × ⁵⁄₃₂ inches
Plywood board veneered with abebay for the side pieces and the door: 43⁵⁄₁₆ × 48 × ½ inches
Reinforcement board for the bracket base of the piece of furniture.

1. Drawings done to scale. Full-sized details are used to trace patterns for making the curved parts of the piece.

2. The pattern is used to trace the outlines of the various pieces on the wood. This photograph depicts the parts that correspond to the top molding.

3. All of the curved pieces are cut out with the band saw, very carefully, along the lines.

4. Then, shaping of the curved profile is finished with a rasp.

5. A vertical shaper is used to make the moldings using cutting blades of the required shape.

6. The simpler molding used for the base of the cabinet is cut out in the same manner on the same machine. The moldings are formed by passing the wood through the blades several times.

7. The pieces that make up the molded base are made next. Using a marking gauge, the required shape and depth are marked on the wood for planing.

8. The pentagon-shaped pieces are created on the planer. The side fence has been tilted to achieve the desired angle.

9. The side fence of the planer is returned to a right angle and the woodworker continues working on the pentagon-shaped pieces until the desired shape is achieved.

10. The square and pentagon legs are cut to the same height as the molded baseboards. The plywood board veneered with abebay wood is placed over it.

11. The legs and the molded base parts are brushed with glue and attached with screws. The base and the plywood board are also glued and attached with dowels to some additional reinforcing pieces, which create a larger contact surface.

3

4

5

6

7

8

9

10

11

12. Screws are inserted in the angled pieces to exert more pressure while the white glue dries.

13. The finished base of the corner display cabinet.

14. To make the door and the sides of the lower module of the display cabinet, the joints of the posts and the crosspieces are marked.

15. With a circular saw, the tenons of the joints of the crosspieces are cut.

16. Cuts at 45-degree angles are made to be able to assemble the moldings; the pieces are shaped and the excess wood removed with a tenon saw.

17. The mortises of the posts are cut. The drill press is used for this task.

18. After the joints and the moldings are made with the milling machine, the wood is trimmed with a chisel so that the pieces will fit into the crosspieces.

19. Unassembled and assembled side pieces showing how the panels fit into the grooves of the frame.

20. The parts that make up the door with the arched top.

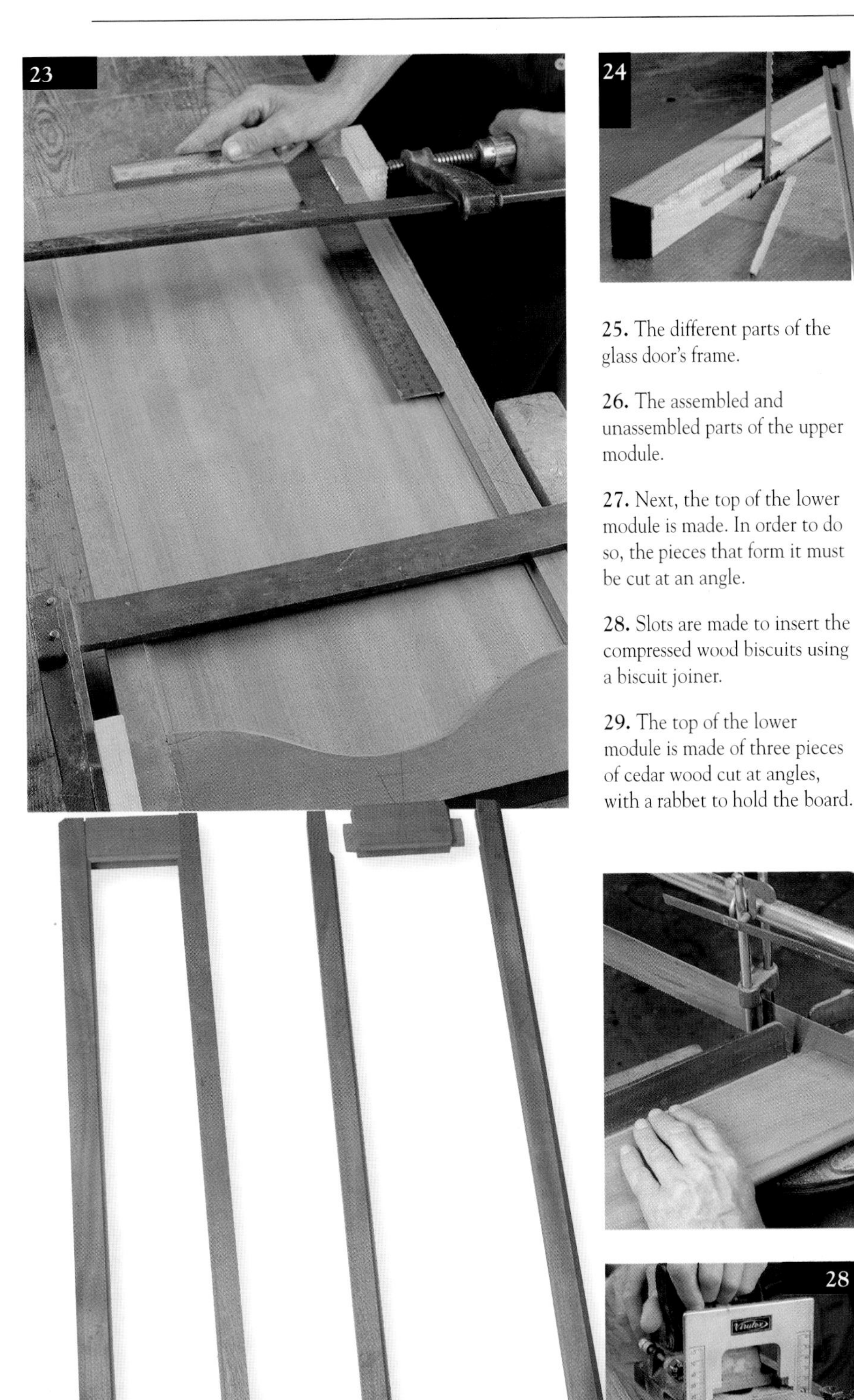

25. The different parts of the glass door's frame.

26. The assembled and unassembled parts of the upper module.

27. Next, the top of the lower module is made. In order to do so, the pieces that form it must be cut at an angle.

28. Slots are made to insert the compressed wood biscuits using a biscuit joiner.

29. The top of the lower module is made of three pieces of cedar wood cut at angles, with a rabbet to hold the board.

21. Before the door is attached to the side units, the inside edges of the moldings and the crosspieces should be sanded. The design of the tenon used for the assembly will also hide gaps in the joint.

22. Glue is brushed on the pieces. A hammer and a piece of wood can make the assembly easier.

23. The pieces are held together with clamps; the posts and the crosspieces should be squared.

24. Next, the woodworker proceeds as before to make the door and the sides of the upper module, with the exception of the rabbet, which will later accommodate a wood strip.

30. Glue is applied to the ends of the pieces cut at angles, and the compressed wood biscuits are inserted in them.

31. Glue is applied to the rabbet, then the board is put in place and the assembly is held together with screws.

32. The next step is to build the frame of the top unit of the cabinet. This is joined with glue and wood splines.

33. Screws are used to strengthen the parts that form the framework.

34. The top part of the frame is smoothed with a rasp so the board that will cover the piece of furniture will fit properly.

35. The moldings are attached to the frame with white glue and screws.

36. In order to shape the board that will cover the top part of the cabinet, it must first undergo a treatment of moistening and pressure. To do this the woodworker should have a piece of rope and several strips of wood to be used as a tourniquet.

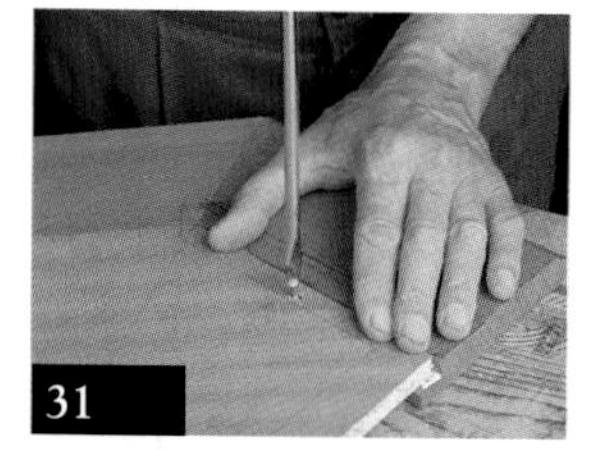

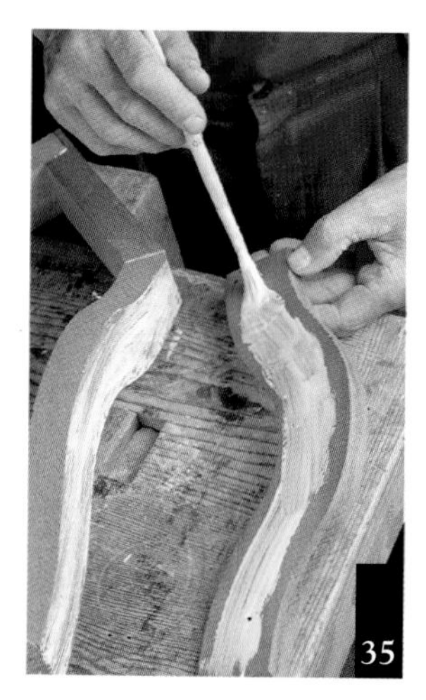

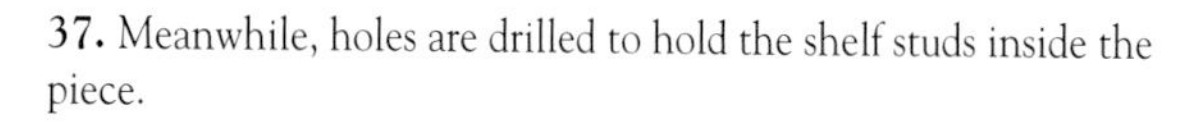
37. Meanwhile, holes are drilled to hold the shelf studs inside the piece.

38. Once the board has been shaped, it is cut to fit the top frame, to which it is bonded with white glue. At the same time, pressure is applied to the pieces with clamps to guarantee a good bond.

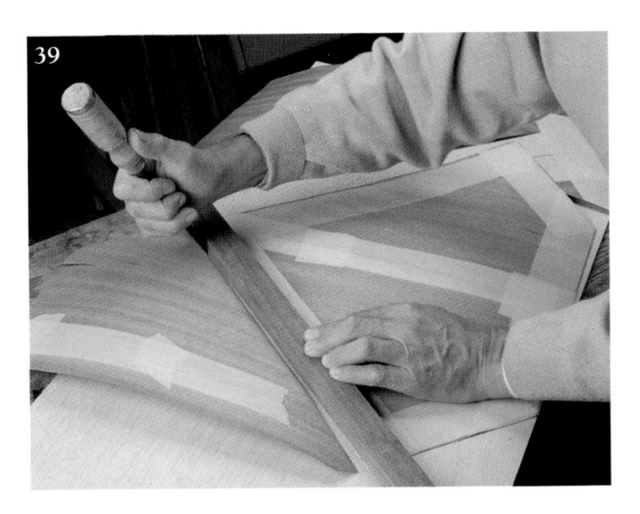

39. A veneer of abebay wood is prepared to cover the board at the top of the cabinet.

40. With the help of a scraping blade, contact cement is applied to the board and veneer.

41. After the contact cement has been applied to both pieces and it feels dry to the touch, the two pieces are bonded together.

42. Pressure is applied evenly to the veneer with the palms of the hands.

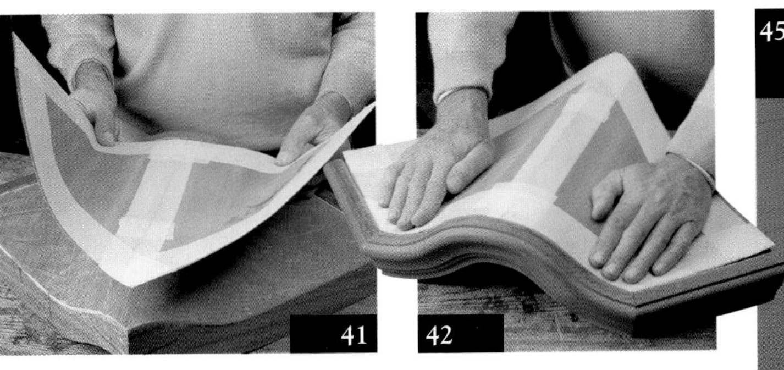

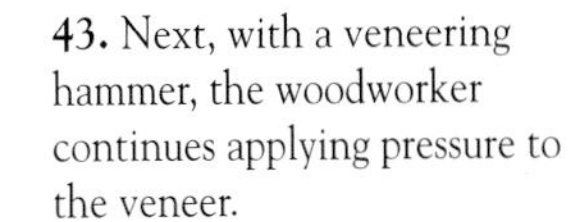

43. Next, with a veneering hammer, the woodworker continues applying pressure to the veneer.

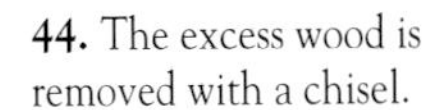

44. The excess wood is removed with a chisel.

45. We can now proceed with the assembly of all the parts of the corner cabinet. The assembly will be done without glue so the pieces can be taken apart. Before the final assembly takes place, all the pieces must be sanded thoroughly.

46. Now the different pieces can be glued together. The glue is applied to the holes of the joints with a thin brush.

47. A hammer and a block of wood are used to fit the pieces together.

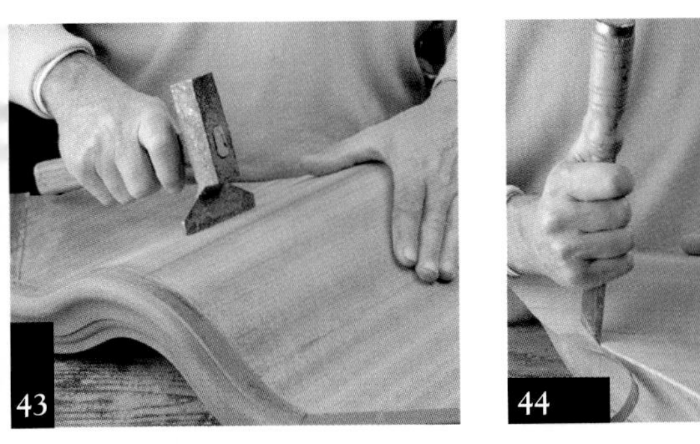

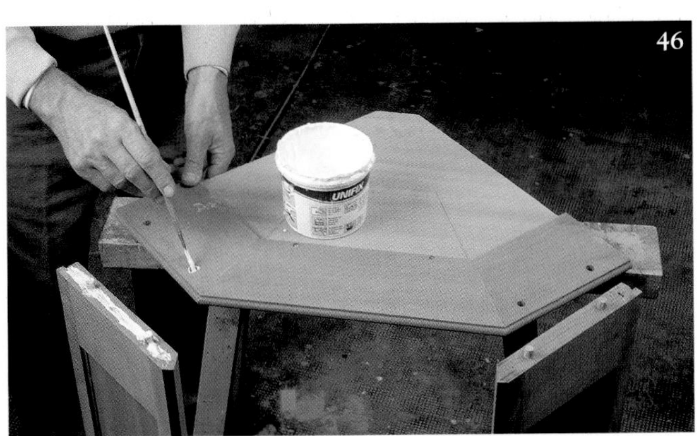

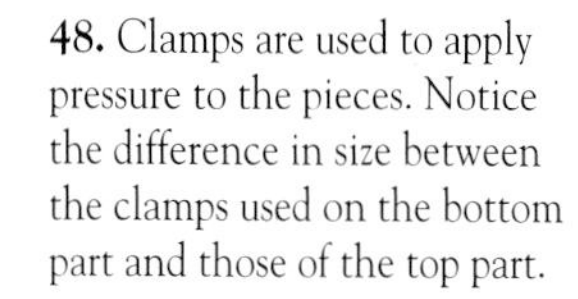

48. Clamps are used to apply pressure to the pieces. Notice the difference in size between the clamps used on the bottom part and those of the top part.

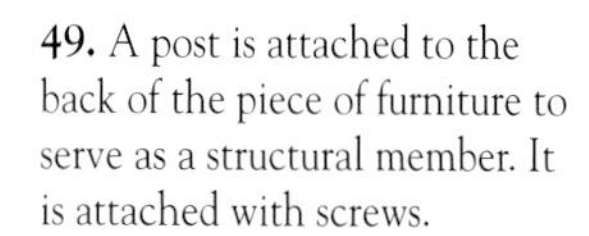

49. A post is attached to the back of the piece of furniture to serve as a structural member. It is attached with screws.

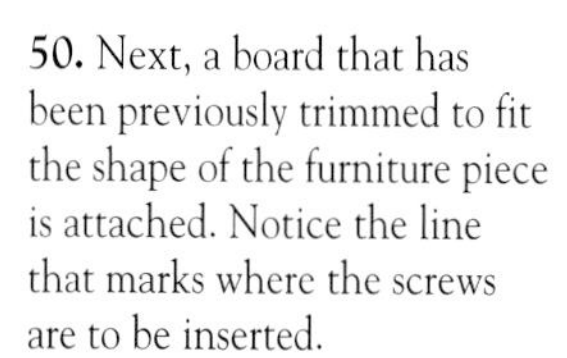

50. Next, a board that has been previously trimmed to fit the shape of the furniture piece is attached. Notice the line that marks where the screws are to be inserted.

51. The locations of the hinges are then marked and wood is removed so they can be inset. The hinges are attached to the doors first.

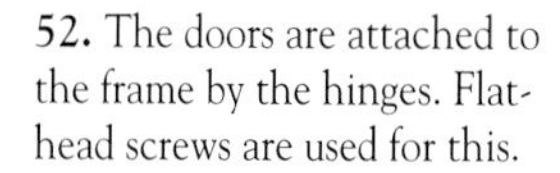

52. The doors are attached to the frame by the hinges. Flat-head screws are used for this.

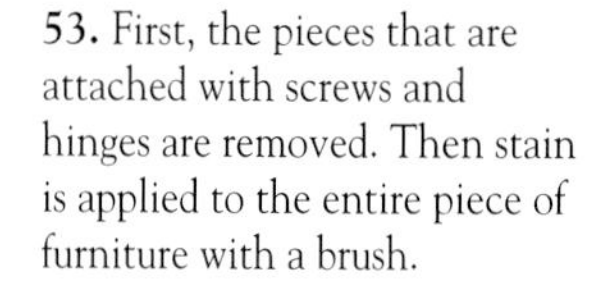

53. First, the pieces that are attached with screws and hinges are removed. Then stain is applied to the entire piece of furniture with a brush.

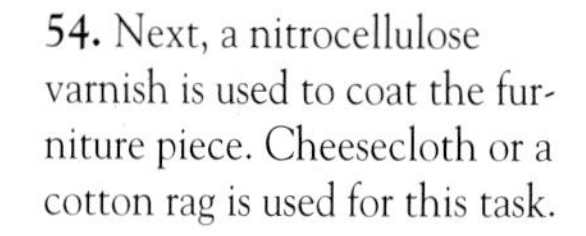

54. Next, a nitrocellulose varnish is used to coat the furniture piece. Cheesecloth or a cotton rag is used for this task.

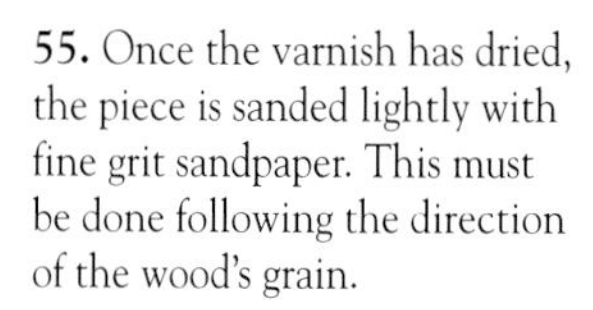

55. Once the varnish has dried, the piece is sanded lightly with fine grit sandpaper. This must be done following the direction of the wood's grain.

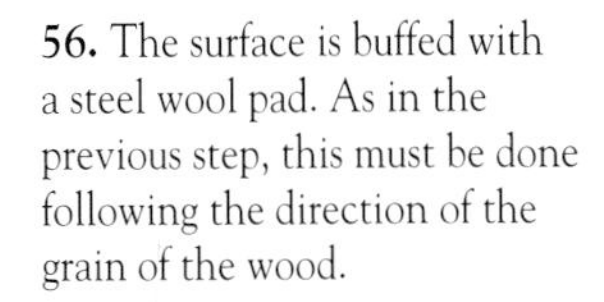

56. The surface is buffed with a steel wool pad. As in the previous step, this must be done following the direction of the grain of the wood.

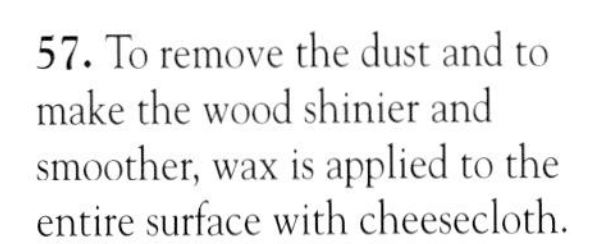

57. To remove the dust and to make the wood shinier and smoother, wax is applied to the entire surface with cheesecloth.

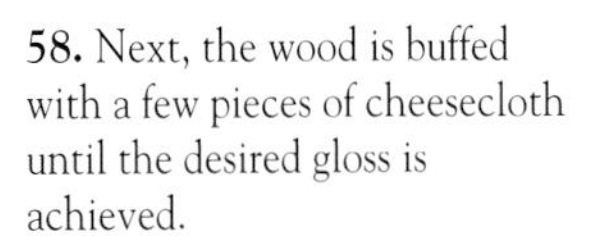

58. Next, the wood is buffed with a few pieces of cheesecloth until the desired gloss is achieved.

59. The pieces of glass are put in place. A blanket has been placed over the worktable so as not to damage the finish of the wood.

60. The glass is held against the posts and crosspieces with small strips of wood and small nails. The hammer must be moved across the glass piece very carefully to avoid breaking it.

61. The door pulls are attached with screws very carefully, because the screwdriver could damage the wood.

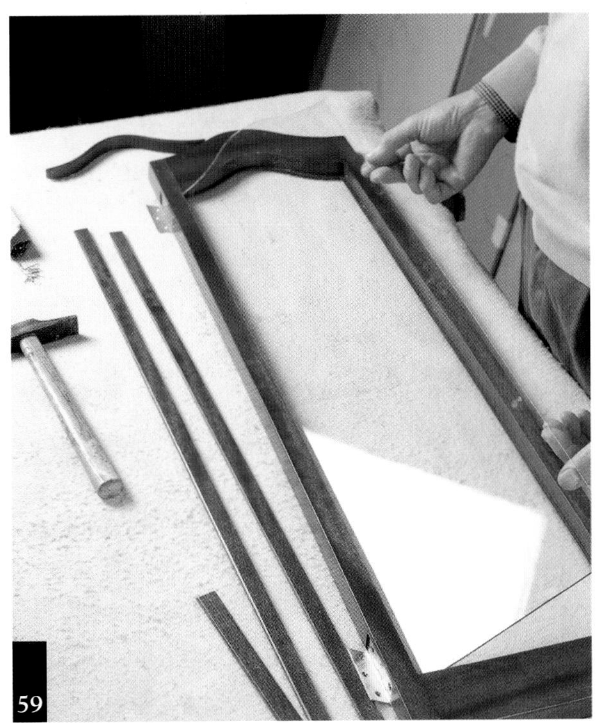

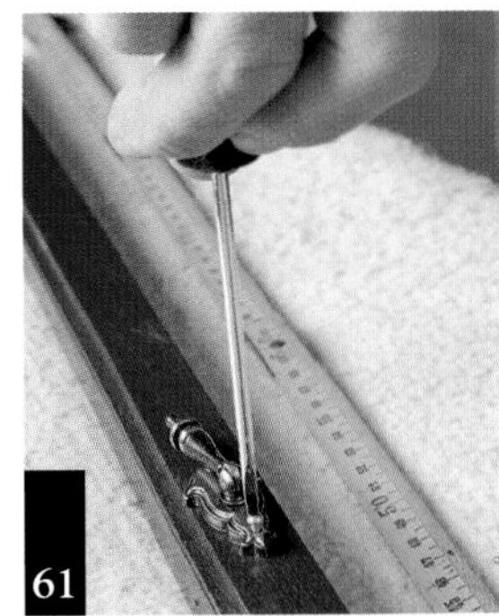

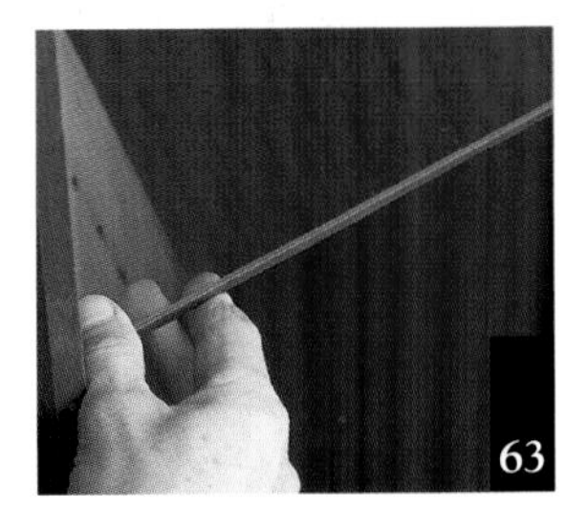

62. The doors are put back in place.

63. Finally, the glass shelves are placed inside by resting them on brass shelf studs.

64. The corner display cabinet completely finished.

GLOSSARY

Awl. Steel tool with a point on one end. Used for making holes and marking parts.
Bench dog. Wood stop inserted into holes on top of the workbench used for holding wood pieces in place.
Biscuit. A small part made of compressed wood fibers, circular or oval in shape, which is used to join wood pieces.
Boards. Rectangular pieces of wood whose dimensions can vary from 1 × 12 inches (3 × 30 cm) to 4 × 12 inches (10 × 30 cm).
Brad. A small nail.
Brush. A tool with long soft fibers attached to a handle, used for applying adhesive or stain and varnish.
Carpenter's glue. White glue.
Carve (to). To shape and reduce a piece of wood.
Chisel. Steel tool used to carve wood.
Clamp. Metal tool that is used to hold a piece on the workbench or hold parts together under pressure.
Contact cement. A type of adhesive used for bonding parts that are difficult to clamp or hold in place. It is also used for bonding melamine and for veneering wood.
Corner block. A triangular piece of wood used to reinforce chairs.
Curing. Process by which an adhesive's watery paste acquires consistency.
Cut up (to). To cut the wood into smaller pieces.
Dimensions. The vertical and horizontal measurements of a cross section of a piece of wood.
Dowel. Small cylindrical wood piece that is used to hold and reinforce joints.
Dye. Substance or color that is used for staining. One of the best-known natural substances is walnut pigment, a coloring agent that is obtained from the walnut shell and that is diluted in water to mimic the color of the walnut wood. Artificial stains are called aniline dyes.
End grain. Surface that results from sawing a piece of wood perpendicularly to the fibers.
Fiber. Dry sap vein that follows the length of the trunk of the tree.
Finish. The final treatment that is applied to a piece of furniture or wood object.
Grain. The fiber of the wood.
Join (to). To assemble two pieces of wood using some version of a mortise and tenon.
Miter. Right-angle joint formed by parts of a molding or board.
Molding. Special wood strips used to hold a glass panel in a frame or to protect and decorate the piece of furniture.
Mortise. Rectangular joint or hole made in a piece of wood for joining with a tenon.
Plane (to). To remove the roughest parts of the wood.
Rabbet. Channel in which the edge of a piece is fitted.
Rabbit-skin glue. An adhesive of animal origin, made from the hide and bones of the animal. In the past, it was often used for bonding pieces of wood. Nowadays it is not used very much, except for veneering wood. It is available in the form of flakes or fine granules, which must be dissolved in hot water in a double boiler.
Scraper. Metal tool with sharp edges, and sometimes with teeth, which is used to clean surfaces and to remove old paint. It is also used for spreading glue evenly on a flat surface.
Scraping. Method of smoothing or polishing wood before finishing it with varnish or wax.
Spline. A long, thin piece of wood inserted into grooves in two boards to help join them.
Strip. Narrow piece of wood whose dimensions measure about 1½ × 3 inches (4 × 8 cm).
Tenon. The end of a piece of wood made thinner than the rest, which allows it to be inserted into a matching hole in another piece of wood.
Tongue. Tenon.
Varnish. A solution of gum or resin in a solvent that, when applied on a surface, dries and forms a coating that is more or less glossy, transparent, and waterproof.
Veneer. A very thin sheet of wood that is applied as a decorative covering.
Veneered. A piece of wood that is covered with veneer.
Wax. An animal or vegetable substance that is used as a finishing coat on wood surfaces.
White glue (also known as carpenter's glue). A polyvinyl acetate adhesive. It is one of the least expensive and easiest adhesives to use. It is excellent for all-purpose use and it is nontoxic.

METRIC CONVERSION CHART

As a general rule, when converting inches to centimeters, multiply the amount of inches by **2.54**.

Inches	Centimeters	Inches	Centimeters	Inches	Centimeters
1	2.54	10	25.40	35	88.90
2	5.08	11	27.94	40	101.60
3	7.62	12	30.48	45	114.30
4	10.16	13	33.02	50	127.00
5	12.70	14	35.56	55	139.70
6	15.24	15	38.10	60	152.40
7	17.78	20	50.80	65	165.10
8	20.32	24	60.96	70	177.80
9	22.86	30	76.20		